GOOD GUN
BAD GUY

*BILL, IT'S GREAT TO KNOW YOU —
KEEP UP THE GREAT WORK YOU DO — . .*

GOOD GUN BAD GUY

Behind the Lies of the Anti-Gun Radical

By Dan Wos

IRON CAT
PUBLISHING
SARATOGA SPRINGS, NY

Good Gun Bad Guy

First Edition Library of Congress Cataloging-in-Publication Data

Good Gun Bad Guy | Daniel J. Wos – 1st ed.

ISBN-13: 978-0692645079
ISBN-10: 0692645071

Edited by Bill Dolan
Foreword by Jan Morgan
Cover design by Dan Wos
Photo credit: Lou DiGesare

Iron Cat Publishing
PO BOX 3331
Saratoga Springs, NY 12866
www.goodgunbadguy.com

Printed in the United States of America

10 9 8 7 6 5 4 3 2

For my Dad, Walter J. Wos

Good Gun Bad Guy

"A well regulated Militia, being necessary to the security of a free State, the right of the people to keep and bear Arms, shall not be infringed."

Good Gun Bad Guy

TABLE OF CONTENTS

Good Gun Bad Guy

FOREWORD

By Jan Morgan

Thirty seconds. It was the last commercial break before I would be live, on national television. The producer with Fox Business Network alerted me in my ear piece that they were coming straight to me at the end of the break.

There I sat, clock ticking, in a studio in Arkansas, linked to a network facility in New York, about to engage in a live debate with a gun hating radical from a national anti-gun organization.

I wasn't the least bit nervous. After all, the facts are on my side in this issue. This should be a very quick, one sided debate. I was prepared to mop the floor with my guest who was likely armed for debate with nothing more than emotion based rants.

I was correct. This debate was quick and one sided. HER side. Once my opposition began talking, she never stopped. The anchor interrupted her more than once to give me a chance to respond, however, the moment I began to speak, my opposition would begin raising her voice, talking over me and spewing her propaganda.

The segment ended. The anchor apologized for the rude, obnoxious behavior of the other guest and I left wondering what had just happened. I spent the limo ride home second guessing myself. Should I have become angry and raised my voice above the radical to see if I could win the shouting match? I was expecting to engage in intelligent civilized discourse with another adult on the merits of the 2nd Amendment and why her personal irrational fears of guns do not trump my right to bear arms.

Instead, we both walked away accomplishing nothing. Hours later, after re-hashing what happened, I realized why I failed in this encounter. I did not know my enemy. Isn't that the first rule of war?

The reason the gun hater didn't let me speak is because she was afraid... afraid of guns... afraid of my facts... afraid of failing her organization. FEAR drives people to strange places where simple logic and facts do not play a role in thought processes.

If only Dan Wos had written this book six months earlier, I would have known exactly who my opposition is, where she's coming from, and how to help her see the situation with logic rather than fear and anger.

The two sides in the 2nd Amendment debate have been arguing the same talking points for decades. The fact that we are still debating the issue, rather than putting it to rest is a pretty good indicator that neither side is making much progress in swaying people to their side.

This book is going to be my "go to" book for successful engagement with Anti-Gun Radicals. There have been books, documentaries, and blogs about gun rights, complete with statistics and talking points, however, there has never to my knowledge, been a book written about the mindset of those who want to take away our gun rights.

Dan Wos takes us inside the minds of these people. He does this in a way than no one else can because he was once ONE OF THEM.

Every gun owning American needs to own and read this book. It will help you understand the motives and explore the reasoning behind these radical gun grabbers. Knowing and understanding them is the first step to defeating them.

Dan Wos was transformed. He is now one of us. My hope is that millions of gun owners will read this book and become better warriors on the 2nd Amendment front. A few of us on the national level, fighting this battle, are not enough.

Never underestimate the power of intelligent gun owners in large numbers. If we all do our part in our own communities to begin reshaping the views of our local anti-gun friends and neighbors, we will win this battle nationally. This book is your training manual.

LET'S GET BUSY!

~Jan Morgan,
FOX News Analyst
NRA Certified Firearms Instructor

Good Gun Bad Guy

PREFACE

I've always been fascinated by how people make decisions in life. What causes one person to take a specific action in a certain circumstance, while another person takes a completely different action under the same circumstance. Thoughts trigger actions, but beliefs germinate thoughts. It's a person's beliefs that ultimately create their life path, their viewpoint and where they focus their passion.

This book is for those who believe that personal defense is not only a right but a duty. It's a book written not to boost the morale of Pro-Gunners but to help define the thought process of the Anti-Gunners. Understanding their beliefs will better help us help them see the situation with logic rather than reactive fear or anger.

It would seem that the Constitution is under attack by bureaucrats and others doing everything they can to restrict the ability of good Americans to defend themselves and their families. The support for gun-restrictions by left-wing politicians (including the President) has been fueled by dishonest statistics, misleading rhetoric and unethical media practices. Although it has been a very difficult task defending our rights, real Americans in support of the right to bear arms have come out in droves. It has truly been a patriotic movement and a very proud (yet tedious) fight for those who believe in personal liberty under the stars and stripes.

Many books have been written in support of gun rights and many patriotic celebrities have put their reputations on the line in defense of law-abiding gun owners across this country. I hold great respect and admiration for them.

Good Gun Bad Guy

I have noticed that although the books, movies, and other media that have come out in support of American liberty and gun rights have been necessary, there has been an absence of talk on the topic of the mindset of those who want to take away the rights of the American people. I felt a need to expose the motives and explore the thought process of the radical gun-grabbing "Americans" that walk among us. It's important to understand the motives of those who constantly assault you because it helps in understanding how to defeat them and/or help them. There has never been a stronger need than now to reverse course and re-implement healthy, traditional American values into our society. I hope that we Americans (those who believe in and abide by the Constitution) use this time wisely and take back our country from those who are mistreating, misrepresenting and disrespecting it. Once our rights and liberties are gone, they are gone forever. I know there are millions of people who are not willing to let that happen. To you I write this book.

Does the photo on the cover of this book cause a reaction in you? What kind of reaction? Was it one of fear, curiosity, anger, excitement, comfort, or something else? Have you ever stopped to ask yourself why you feel a certain way when confronted with a stimulating image, sound, odor or taste? Throughout Good Gun Bad Guy we will explore what causes these feelings and why we do what we do, but most importantly we will explore the mind of the Anti-Gunner without their consent.

I understand there are some people who respect the 2nd Amendment but would like to see more restrictions placed on guns because they still blame violence on guns and not the people using them. To those people, I say, there are plenty of laws already. Maybe enforcing the laws already on the books would be a good focus point for you. Then, there are those who just want guns to go away forever. They are the ones who do not want to hear logic, don't care what anyone has to say in defense of the 2nd Amendment and only believe the radical anti-gun views that are spoon-fed to them through their TV screen and social media feed. They are the focus of this book. They are the ones I endearingly refer to as the Anti-2nd Amendment Radicals. To them I say, we will fight like angry hornets to preserve and defend our rights if we must, and we will not negotiate. The Anti-2nd Radicals will not even be given a seat at the negotiating table because the 2nd Amendment is not up for debate.

When I refer to an Anti-Gunner, I am referring to a person who in general does not like guns, has a great fear of guns, has no real experience with guns and would prefer they be removed from society. An Anti-Gunner generally believes that guns are the cause of shootings. An Anti-Gunner may still have respect for the Constitution and the rights of the people but would not be opposed to heavy gun restrictions. An Anti-Gunner may not necessarily want to see people lose their Constitutional rights and they are not freedom-hating statists. They just want to feel safe and may have innocently been misled by rhetoric from Barack Obama, Chuck Schumer, Hillary Clinton, Diane Feinstein and the likes thereof.

An Anti-2nd Amendment Radical has most of the same traits as an Anti-Gunner but would also like to see the 2nd Amendment repealed. These are the people who fight hard and do everything they can to destroy the 2nd Amendment. Anti-2nd Amendment Radicals would love to see gun owners completely disarmed. They welcome complete government control over all guns and they claim anyone with a gun is potentially dangerous. They denounce and deny the words in the 2nd Amendment and they would cheer in the streets should the 2nd Amendment be repealed and gun owners finally under complete control of a Government they put in office. Anti-2nd Amendment Radicals do not entertain pro-gun statistics, philosophies or the rights of the people under the Constitution. They only want to win the fight against gun owners to ultimately see them unarmed and helpless. They want control, they want no armed opposition and they know they are lying.

If you smiled while reading that, you might be an Anti-2nd Amendment Radical. Good Gun Bad Guy focuses on this group of people.

Anti-Gunners will benefit from this book because they will get insight from a source they would not normally hear from. The information here is not what you see on CNN. The Pro-Gunners will benefit from this book because they will gain a window into the minds of those who want to see their rights taken away. Anti-2nd Amendment Radicals will not like this book at all, as it shines the light of truth on them.

Many books have been written about gun laws, gun statistics, and the rights of gun owners, but none have been written about what is going on in the minds of those who believe guns should be eliminated from society....until now.

ACKNOWLEDGMENTS

Many people have had influence on my life in ways that have helped me move forward. I can't possibly name them all, but I can name the most influential people with respect to the topic of guns and how they relate to my life. Without these people I may not have followed the path I took that led to this book.

First, I would like to thank my Dad, Walter Wos for introducing me to firearms in a way that was honest. He also showed me the importance they play in our lives on many levels. Without seeing the passion and respect he had for guns, I may not have developed the same understanding I now have.

My wife Sue for trusting me and adjusting her beliefs to accept and appreciate my transition into gun ownership. It's a family commitment and her adaptation was crucial. I respect the difficulty she may have had especially knowing that it was totally foreign to her.

The guys who trained, advised and helped me understand the responsibility that goes along with gun ownership; Bill Dolan, Mark Sorenson, Vic Ferrante, Rocco Mazzarello, Mark Dobert, Larry Harland, Kevin Zacharewicz, Leo Nicotera, Pete Conprotst and Kyle Murphy. You may have no idea (until now) how helpful you were.

And the people who endure endless backlash from the political left, yet still fight tirelessly in the public eye to raise awareness and protect our right to keep and bear arms; Wayne LaPierre, Chris Cox, Jan Morgan, Ted Nugent, Dana Loesch, Jeff Cooper, Sheriff David Clarke, Glenn Beck, Donald Trump, Sarah Palin, Ted Cruz, Larry Pratt, Rand Paul, John Lott, Mark Levin, Mike Lee, Sean Hannity, Rick Perry, Oliver North, David Keene, Dudley Brown, Ben Shapiro, Chuck Norris, Michael Savage, Colion Noir, S.E. Cupp, Michael

Berry, Julianne Versnel, Gary Sinise, Ice T, John Bolton, Kurt Russell, Erich Pratt

INTRODUCTION

When I was a kid, my Dad took me out hunting and target shooting. He loved it. Me, not so much. It just wasn't my thing. I tried, but just wasn't interested. I mean, I didn't dislike guns and I wasn't scared of them. I just wasn't all that interested. When he would buy a new pistol, he would show it to me and I could tell he loved these things. Of course I showed interest and they were actually kinda cool but I was more interested in my guitar so I never really jumped on board with the whole "gun thing." My Dad would even build his own rifles. I remember going down to the basement where he would be assembling old muzzle loader replicas, oiling the wood, staining and just working on these things with such passion. I would later understand that passion and recognize it in myself.

I was always aware of sort of an "anti-gun" niche of people and they never really mattered to me because I never had a vested interest in guns throughout most of my life. I just thought, "some people like guns and some don't. So what?" It wasn't until later in life that I started to see the importance and value in firearms. I also became very clear on the way fear gets attached to guns.

One night my wife and I were coming out of a late movie at the mall theater in Albany, NY and as we were walking down the dark sidewalk to the back parking lot we ran into a situation. Sue was walking down the center of the sidewalk and I was to her right (closest to the curb). Walking directly toward her, also in the center of the sidewalk was this guy. This angry looking guy, about six foot five, maybe two hundred and fifty pounds, wearing a hoodie so I could barely see his face. But I could tell he was not happy and he was not moving to the side. Keep in mind this sidewalk was plenty wide enough to accommodate three people from side to side. When you recognize a situation like this, it is hard to rationalize it away because our "fight or flight" mechanism kicks in when we sense some sort of danger. As much as some people will tell you not to judge people or assume they are bad and looking for trouble, it can be a challenge to keep your internal thoughts calm in a time when you sense danger. I don't care who you are; you get scared because you don't know the outcome. But you must stay rational and when you are prepared to defend yourself, the fear is decreased.

So, as this creep gets closer to Sue, walking straight toward her, I'm boiling over with adrenaline and trying to keep calm. *"He is not moving to the side,"* I thought. *"He's going to run right into her."* When he got about three feet away from her, she quickly moved to her right and he bumped her so hard in the shoulder that she bumped into me and knocked me off the curb. We both almost fell over and he kept walking down the center of the sidewalk like he owned it. This was no accident. He was clearly looking for trouble and trying to get a reaction out of me.

I turned around still holding her hand and was just about ready to lay into this asshole, but before the words came out, visions of my wife, my son, my great life and everything I've worked so hard to build flashed before my eyes. I had a moment of reality and realized that it's not worth it to put everything at risk. To be honest, I didn't want to get hurt. Most importantly, I didn't want my wife to get hurt. And if something tragic were to happen, I didn't want my son to be alone. How did I know what this guy was capable of? The truth is, I didn't. Somehow I had this moment of clarity and we slowly walked to the car as I bit my lip. To be clear, had I been carrying that night I would have had even more reason to keep my mouth shut and keep walking but if this guy decided he wanted a bigger piece of me I would have at least been able to protect myself and my wife.

Sue and I got into the car and were silent for a few minutes. I slowly put the key in the ignition. I turned to look at her, feeling the most shameful, irresponsible and incapable I have ever felt. I told her I was sorry. I was sorry I put her in a situation like that. I was sorry that I might not have been able to defended her against this monster if a situation had arisen. I was sorry I was unable to protect and defend one of the two most important people in my life. I realized in that moment that life is vulnerable and as a man it is my responsibility to take care of and protect my family. That night I did not and I was ashamed.

Throughout my life, I've seen some wild things, done some wild things and been in some situations that...well, let's just say it's a miracle I'm here. But I'm a bit older now. I'd like to think I'm wiser and beyond the point in my life that I want to be rolling around on the ground exchanging punches with anyone. I told Sue in the car that night, that from now on, as long as she was with me I would never let her be put in a situation where she was defenseless again. I told her I was getting a gun.

Now, keep in mind, Sue didn't know the first thing about guns. She had never been around them and held the belief that most media outlets love to propagate; the misconception that guns are bad and only kill people. So it took some persuading and reassuring to help her feel comfortable, first with the idea, then with the physicality of actual guns in the house and one in my belt.

As a gun owner there is a completely different understanding of what we are capable of and the responsibility we have that we didn't have before. People who carry are much more likely to avoid the situation and have a different view of situations with respect to reactions and emotions. A lot changes and interactions are handled completely different now because the fear level is different and the understanding of your ability is different. It's even more crucial to avoid any confrontation whatsoever.

Through the process of getting re-trained, licensing, educating myself on all the models and features new handguns have, ammo options, safes, holsters and all the safety procedures I started to gain a passion for these interesting devices. Frankly, they're pretty cool. Mechanically they are amazing and I literally can't wait to get to the range. Lucky for me, I have some really informative, articulate and skillful friends who walked me through the entire process and took great care in training me and holding me accountable to every aspect of the process. The friends I have met that shoot are some of the most respectful and responsible people I know. The interesting thing that non-gun owners may not be aware of is that there is a mental piece that goes along with gun ownership and a responsibility that many people will never understand. I now understand what Dad was talking about. The entire process of embracing the gun culture and working through my wife's emotions and beliefs (as well as my own) has been an enlightening experience. When we are now in a potentially dangerous location, she asks if I'm carrying. Why do you think she asks? When I tell her, "Of course I am," how do you think she feels?

The whole reason I am writing this is to get to the psychological piece. I know there are some people reading this that will never allow themselves to accept gun ownership and that's ok but by recognizing the fear of guns and addressing the fact that most of what we see in the media depicts guns as killing devices, we may start to be able to see through that propaganda and understand the value in preserving the precious gift of life.

1. FEAR OF GUNS

"Guns scare me, so I don't think you should be allowed to own them."

"Why do you carry a gun around? What are you so afraid of?" These are typical condescending questions we get from the Anti-2nd Amendment Radicals with respect to our gun ownership. It's asked with a sarcastic tone in an attempt to make the whole idea of the 2nd Amendment seem ridiculous. It's a way for them to line up with Barack Obama's attempts at making gun owners appear unreasonable and childish. His most infamous and divisive comment was: *"They get bitter, they cling to guns or religion."* Never missing an opportunity, President Obama said this to imply that people of faith irrationally *cling* to their Bibles for comfort and gun owners irrationally *cling* to their guns for a false sense of security.

In an attempt to defend our beliefs and justify our actions, we sarcastically respond to the *"What are you so afraid of?"* question by saying things like *"I'm not afraid of anything, I carry a gun."* But the truth is, it's a difficult question to answer because we don't really know. Any number of things could happen that would justify owning or carrying a gun. We really don't know what situations we may find ourselves in next week, tomorrow or five minutes from now. The Anti-2nd Amendment Radicals know this so they use the question *"What are you so afraid of?"* with a smirk and as a way of playing Gotcha.

Fear is engrained in the Anti-Gunner's philosophy. But not in the way you might think. The average Anti-Gunner represents a portion of our society that is ill-informed and willing to take on beliefs as long as they are packaged in a way that is easy to comprehend and don't take a lot of thought or in-depth soul searching. He or she is generally scared to death of guns and will embrace any ideas that support and justify that fear; because what would it mean about them if they were to realize their fear of guns was irrational? They believe that guns themselves are dangerous because they have been programmed to believe that and they would like to see guns go away. Rather than acquiring data and getting trained in the safe use of firearms, most condemn, ridicule and criminalize guns and gun owners. They have been spoon-fed hand-picked data while simultaneously being bombarded with images of death and destruction. The data and images are always artfully crafted in a way that discourages critical thinking on the topic of guns.

What should we expect? Not everyone has the wherewithal to go against common opinion (or what is made to appear to be common opinion) in an effort to find truth and support ethics and morality. The media and government string-pullers recognize this about human nature and see this as an opportunity to manipulate public opinion. To them, this is an easy way to recruit support for their cause and they use it to its full capacity. The embarrassing thing is watching our fellow Americans, friends and even family members fall for it.

For a period of time I was one of those people. I believed the rhetoric and allowed myself to be manipulated to the point that I despised guns and had no time for anyone who would own them. This was true even though I came from an environment where guns were present and even after having gone hunting and target shooting as a kid. I'm here to tell you that the rhetoric and brainwashing works. Fortunately for my family and me logic prevailed and as soon as I started to question the validity of the Anti-2nd Radical's chatter, their house of cards started to fall. I soon realized that the reason I started to become fearful of guns was simply a lack of data and an insertion of misleading information & images by the media & fear-mongers. That's just how our brains work. Beliefs grow out of data that we acquire along the way and on a consistent basis. As soon as I started to get real data on the topic, their fear campaign became transparent. They use fear to seduce and I started to see their whole platform fall apart as common sense took over.

The more I studied the gun culture and dissected the words of the media outlets and some politicians, the more I was able to recognize the misleading nature and ill-intent they have. I started to clearly see the zombie-like anti-gun supporters jumping on the opportunity to push their agenda every time a new school shooting occurred. I am at the point now where although it still annoys me, I actually feel a level of compassion for the misled minions because they believe with their heart and soul that they are fighting the good fight. It's even more difficult for them to break free from the mind manipulation now because fear is being used against them in the most strategic and powerful ways that it has ever been used. When the media is strategically controlled by politics, finding the truth requires active searching, and many people are simply unwilling to put forth the effort to seek it out. So they watch whatever is on the tube at the dinner table.

When the media is in on creating an alternate reality it is very hard for people to see the truth. Once people are indoctrinated into the fear camp, anything that supports their existing beliefs will strengthen the fear. Anything that contradicts their beliefs is taught to be considered irrelevant or conspiratorial and is encouraged to be discarded.

Fear is the strongest human motivator but it is simply just a lack of necessary data. It is created in the mind and body as a reaction for the purpose of causing one to take action. In some cases it causes

27

non-action. You know the saying "Frozen by fear." The way you can tell that fear is caused by a lack of data is to ask yourself, if in any "fearful" situation would knowing the outcome reduce the feeling of fear? Think about it for a minute. You're scared. Why? Because you don't know what will happen. Once it happens, are you still scared? Take any situation you might be experiencing right now in life that you consider scary or even something you are worried about. What if you had a crystal ball that could tell you exactly how the situation will play out? Now you know the outcome. Are you still scared? If you said yes, ask yourself if there is yet another unknown future outcome still left unanswered related to the situation. The ultimate end result of acquiring necessary data results in the absence of fear. In other words, once you get the data, the fear is gone.

The fear of death is the strongest human motivator. As a matter of fact, we have internal, instinctive mechanisms within us designed to preserve our lives. Should we ever need to access those mechanisms, our bodies and brain take over involuntarily. Adrenaline is activated during extremely stressful or fearful times to give us strength. Clarity and focus can be enhanced during times when crucial decisions need to be made.

Here's an example. I'll use the tried and true "Fight or Flight" and "Tiger" scenario. You're in the jungle and you come face to face with a vicious tiger that has decided to make you his lunch. You're looking directly into the eyes of the beast as he positions himself to pounce. Your "Fight or Flight" kicks in and adrenaline rushes through your body so your muscles have the ability to help you operate at maximum potential. In that moment of terror, you don't know if you will die or escape. You just don't have any way of knowing the outcome. But let's just say that in a split second you are able to see into the future and realize that your friend will shoot the tiger dead in his tracks before it gets a chance to attack you. Now that you know the outcome, are you still scared? Try it with something that is going on in your life right now. What is it right now in life that has you scared, worried or even just concerned? With respect to your situation, what information is missing? Think about it. With any fear there is something left unknown. In your current situation, what "unknown" is causing your concern? Once you realize what is left unknown, answer the question or hypothesize an outcome. When you answer the question or get the relevant data your fear should subside unless you still have unanswered questions or imagined outcomes.

So, what is actually going on in the minds of those who want to see you (Mr. or Mrs. American) unarmed and helpless against an attack? Let's say hypothetically that you are walking through the parking garage to get to your car after working late at the office and you are attacked. I know this could never happen, but if it could, would it be a radical idea to think that having a gun might help you. I'm only being moderately sarcastic to make a point. Let's assume it is possible to be attacked and let's also recognize the fact that in America you do have the right to carry a gun. The beautiful thing about the Bill of Rights is that it points that right out and makes it clear to all. No, you do not have to be at the mercy of another man's violent actions. You and I have the right to defend ourselves. It is a right that is not given to us by another man or group of men. It is an inherent right that exists simply through the conscious awareness of the value of human life. God-given if you choose. It was only written down as a reminder to anyone who would try to take power over you.

I sometimes ask myself if it would be possible to draw up a constitution or a mission statement now, in 2016, that would serve our country. Would it be possible for people to agree on a set of guidelines and standards that would serve us now, and 300 years into the future? My hypothesis is that it could not happen. We would not get past the first sentence. With all the different ideologies, cultures, religions, moral standards and gender identities we have as people in America, creating a document like that would be a herculean task. So what we have instead is a litany of rules, regulations, requirements, limitations, restrictions and laws. It's easy to implement laws because they can be done strategically and affect only a small element of society at a time. Incremental change is much easier to accept than mass regulations that affect the way we live on a broad scale. What we end up with though, are thousands of laws that collectively strangle our freedom.

You can't walk out of your house or even use your own bathroom without being subjected to countless laws and regulations. The amount of water your toilet uses is regulated. Your toothpaste must meet specific standards. The doorknob must meet certain regulations and standards. The light bulbs are restricted. The glass in the windows and the paint on the walls must be made to meet specific guidelines. Even the water must go through strict testing and chemical treatment before you can use it. I'm not saying all regulations are bad but I am pointing out the fact that freedom is given up in their presence. Think about all the rules, regulations and laws you are subjected to just by getting into your car and driving to the gun range. Let's imagine going into the woods and chopping down a pine tree to take back to your home for a Christmas celebration. How many laws do you think you would break?

Why is it that we regulate ourselves to death? Some of it is because we see negative results from specific things so we control that situation and prevent it from happening again in the future. This is understandable and can make good logical sense at times. Traffic lights for instance are a way to make the roads organized and safer but there are other times in which we make rules because we don't trust the actions of our fellow man. We don't believe that under freewill, others will do the right thing. So out of fear and the hopes of preventing anything and everything bad, we regulate and restrict our own freedoms. True, many restrictions are a result of someone taking destructive action or being irresponsible, but rather than correct the problem within the behavior of the person and address the source and thought process of that person, we choose to forcibly control the behavior by threatening each other with penalties. We must now all live by the rules created to control the actions of a few. This is how we trade personal freedom for a sense of safety.

What a certain radical element of our society is trying to do with respect to guns is exactly the same thing. Rather than affectively addressing topics like mental health, drug addiction (both legal and illegal), sexual disorders, radical religious violence, gang violence, family values and responsible parenting, the radicals act out of the need to control society. They believe this will be achieved, in part, by regulating guns. Making it more difficult for good citizens to acquire and use firearms does absolutely nothing to curb violent behavior. It simultaneously puts good people in danger by eliminating their ability to self-defend. Some would argue that while rendering innocent crime-victims helpless, gun restrictions also embolden the criminals because they now know that their opposition has been rendered helpless. This is like declawing the cat because the dog keeps attacking it.

On the surface, when people want to restrict others, it would seem the primary goal is to control. In actuality, rules and laws are exactly that. They are forms of control. The penalty for breaking the law is the leverage. In other words, fear is used to control people. Like I said, some forms of control are ways of organizing and structuring systems and activities that are born out of a desire to create a more efficient society and increase productivity. This is not necessarily motivated by fear. On the other hand, and with guns in particular, the motivation of Anti-Gunners is most definitely fear-based because they believe that by eliminating the gun, they will effectively eliminate the criminal behavior. The criminal behavior is what scares them. Anti-2nd Amendment Radicals however are not necessarily fear based, it would seem. They are primarily driven by the need or desire to control the way people behave. To achieve the goal of changing the way people think about guns and ultimately take them out of society is the primary goal of the Anti-2nd Amendment Radical, but if we look further into the mind of the Anti-2nd Radical and try to understand what drives their need to control, we find yet another underlying source of motivation. It is indeed fear. Yes, again fear is ultimately the motivation, but this time the fear is of not being in control. We are fear-based creatures and will do almost anything if we are scared enough. Feeling safe ultimately becomes our highest priority.

Fear is the greatest tool Anti-2nd Politicians and the media have. They know that lack of data leads to fear so anytime they can create an unknown outcome or worse, a fabricated outcome with unknown effects, they will. They constantly talk about guns getting into the hands of children and how an armed society will lead to the "Wild West" with everyone shooting at each other over the smallest of disagreements. Another fear-favorite is leaving you unsure if the heinous act of violence they just put on your TV screen could happen in your neighborhood. You know they're planting fear when they ask things like, "Could you be next?" Set-ups like that are designed to leave you thinking, *"Well, I don't know. I guess it could happen to me."* The people who create these scenarios are sharp people and we need to recognize that. Anytime a powerful tool like fear can be used to push their agenda, you can bet they will use it. Fear is a human emotion that has been used against us since the beginning of time. Fear is used in the marketing of products every single day.

You may have seen the auto insurance commercial where the

tree falls on the guy's car completely destroying it. By spoon-feeding you that image you are left with the idea that a tree could fall on your car too. I mean, it makes sense right? It's possible. But if you have their insurance you have nothing to worry about because you are covered. So the intent of the commercial is to instill fear in you until you switch insurance companies. They want you to live in fear of trees falling on your car or other catastrophic events happening in your life. Once you purchase the new policy the fear is gone because now you know you are covered. Now you feel safe. Everyone wants to feel safe. The anti-gun media and politicians continuously show people how guns are dangerous and eliminating them from society would (magically?) make everyone safe. They use fear to motivate their anti-gun warriors.

When some people think of guns they instantly think of death and the killing of people. I think it is so sad that these folks have to walk around all day with these destructive, murderous thoughts in their minds, while others are able to recognize the beauty of being able to defend themselves and feel comfortable and safe because they carry a gun. I prefer the feeling of safety to fear and would assume you agree. Now getting back to the fear thing. What is fear? I talk more in-depth on the topic of fear in my book "Defining Success in America." As gun owners, we would be better off understanding that it is fear and lack of knowledge that drives the Anti-Gunners. Understanding that much may serve us better when it comes to educating them and counteracting some of their misguided rhetoric and anger. I also believe that rather than taking a reactive approach to the demonizing of guns, we as gun owners would be much more effective if we were to take a proactive forward moving approach. It seems like we are always defending our rights rather than exercising them. Implementing new firearm related events and options for the public would be a great, proactive start.

Now, with that in mind let's look at how the media portrays guns. We all know that we can turn on any news channel and if they are talking about guns it is never positive and always a story about how guns can kill people. The truth about guns is that they save lives. Ask yourself who you would rather have defend you in the parking lot of a convenience store at two in the morning when a knife wielding maniac is demanding your money. Would you like a soft-spoken person with a kind heart and compassion for the criminal because they think he has been wronged by society or would you prefer an armed police officer. Any logical thinking person would pick the police officer in a time of desperate need (even an Anti-Gunner). Why? Because they have guns. But the problem is, the police officer is never there. Oh, he will be but you may have to give him 5-10 minutes. So in the meantime, you'll have to ask the parking lot maniac to hold on while you call 911, navigate through the dispatcher's questions and then ask your new friend to put his knife down and sit on the curb with you while the two of you wait for the cops to arrive and straighten this misunderstanding out.

Of course I'm being sarcastic! Who in their right mind cannot see the logic here? The fact is, there are a few possible ways this situation can play out.

1. The knife-wielding lunatic can come to his senses and walk away, leaving you unharmed.

2. You can time-travel to another location.

3. The maniac kills you and takes your money.

4. You shoot the criminal and save your own life.

Look, the reality is (whether some people want to see it or not) that it is possible you too may find yourself in a situation like this. Heck, it happens to people every single day. The question you may want to ask yourself is, "Do you want to be able to defend yourself?" Maybe you don't. I guess that's ok too. I *do* want to defend myself. I also want to defend my loved ones and the good people around me. Some that I may have never even met.

I was talking to a guy and I gave him a scenario. I said:

"Let's say hypothetically that you and I are walking through the mall. We don't know each other but it's Christmas time and the place is hopping. People are walking around with their shopping bags full of gifts that they can't wait for their families to open, Jingle Bell Rock is playing on the sound system, (you have your Starbucks latte in your hand) and we happen to be near each other. All of a sudden a masked gunman announces that everyone needs to lie down on the floor as he starts shooting people. I know this could never happen <sarcasm> but if it could...and you now knew that I was armed because you saw me un-holster a handgun as I ducked behind a wall, what thoughts and feelings are rushing through you? If you are a gun owner who decided not to carry that day you would likely be thinking, "I cannot believe I chose today to leave it home. Thank God for that guy- we may have a chance." And if you were previously ambivalent about the subject or anti-gun you would likely be thinking, "Thank God for that guy- we may have a chance."

Sometimes logic does prevail and sometimes people can put their political beliefs aside so they can allow themselves the right to protect their own life. Unfortunately, some need to experience a situation where a gun may have been a useful tool in saving their life before they see the importance of self-defense. Most often, by the

35

time you realize a gun is necessary, it's already too late. I understand that to some, the political narrative is much stronger than the ability to believe that harm can come their way even amidst the countless number of times these horrible situations occur. The general argument among the Anti-2nd Radicals and sometimes even the typical non-gun owner is that the world would be a better place if all guns were removed from society. Although that may or may not be a nice thought with respect to safety, it is fear that drives that thought process. It's the fear of not understanding guns and not knowing how to use them coupled with the misguided fear that guns are dangerous. To latch on to the notion that the world would be a better place if all guns magically "went away" the Anti's must also hold onto the belief that it is a possible scenario. This is complete fantasy on their part and I talk more about this later. Simply stated, it is not possible to remove guns from society. Yes, you may be able to take them form law-abiding citizens, but the Bad Guys will always have them. Gun restrictions only restrict the people who obey the laws. In other words; the Good Guys. Here's the logic that has been falling on deaf ears for decades.

Bad Guys don't pay attention to gun laws. They will still have guns while good people are left unarmed and helpless.

It's really pretty simple and you may be confused as to why everyone doesn't see this logic. But there are specific reasons the Anti-2nd Amendment Radicals can't or won't admit to this simple truth. If they did admit that gun restrictions only affect people who obey laws, they would have to admit that they have been fighting a war in which every battle won gets more innocent people killed. It wouldn't be politically correct to admit that they really don't care how many lives are lost as long as they get what they want. To some, getting what they want means controlling gun owners. Dare I go there and bring to light the notion that some may have become so calloused to death and violence on TV that their mission to prevent others their Constitutional rights far outweighs the value of life? Dare I say that some may not be concerned with the lives of people who lost loved ones because maniacs found their sons, daughters, wives and husbands to be helpless targets? And dare I say that many of the lives lost were a direct result of destructive, selfish anti-gun policies? Well there, I think I just said it.

So why is it that anti-gun policy can create such persistence and passion in Anti-2nd Amendment Radicals? Why do they fight with such ferocity when they know the results put people in danger? How can they look themselves in the mirror after telling us being unarmed and helpless is a better condition than having the ability to defend ourselves? The answer is, they don't believe it but they tell people they believe it and meanwhile they are very happy to have their own guns and bodyguards to defend *their* families. Should any rational person thoughtfully take on the validity of self-defense with no prejudice, logic would take over and force him to admit that when face to face with an armed Bad Guy, the best medicine is a Good Gun. Unlike Anti-2nd Amendment Radicals, Anti-Gunners either avoid the conscious thought process of finding themselves up against an armed Bad Guy, or have been convinced of three things despite the data. They believe guns can actually be removed from society, and that once they are removed (or heavily restricted) The Bad Guy's access will also be limited. They also believe that if they put themselves on the anti-gun side of the battle they will never have to confront the demon that really drives them - their fear of guns.

Some gun owners may argue that being afraid of guns is childish because like anything else, once you get familiar with something and understand how it works, you are no longer afraid of it. In other words, once you get the data, the fear goes away. If you are convinced that guns "go off" all by themselves and gun owners constantly leave their loaded guns in the presence of babies, it's no wonder you would be scared.

My friend Kent and I had lunch at a local restaurant in town while we talked over some real estate investments. The conversation came around to my new carry gun. I found myself showing him a picture of it on my phone when the gun was right in my belt. We laughed because in another time, I would have been able to pull it out and hand it to him. Kent asked me jokingly, *"What response would we get if you put your gun on the table right here in this restaurant, or better yet, we both put our guns on the table?"* The first thing we hypothesized was the fearful reaction the people around us would have to the guns. *"They would hit the floor in sheer panic at the sight of a gun in public,"* I said. Kent noted that many people would most likely scream *"He has a gun!"* We both laughed as we started to discuss the hypothetical situation in detail. Our laughter soon turned to disappointment as we found the topic very interesting and discouraging on several levels. We found ourselves laughing at the ridiculous responses we assumed we would get but it made us think about why people would react this way. Keep in mind this is purely hypothetical because we never did see the actual response, but the conversation opened up our thought process and awareness to just how much society has changed.

We gun owners find a fearful response to guns in the hands of Good Guys to be preposterous, yet we are fully aware that it is a reality among the ill-informed among us. The fear is real to them because they are constantly bombarded with anti-gun rhetoric designed to keep them in a perpetual state of fear. So we try very hard to help them understand that it's not what they think. Kent and I knew that the people in the restaurant that day were much safer for having us there than they would ever have known. We also know that had a situation arisen, we would have protected them. We are the Good Guys. The sad part is, many Anti-Gunners, Non-Gunners and Anti-2nd Radicals consider anyone other than a cop carrying a gun as a danger to society. Lately even cops can't catch a break. This is all due to misleading information and a manipulated narrative by unscrupulous politicians and dishonest media.

The next thing about this hypothetical "guns on the table" scenario was how limited we really have become with respect to our freedoms due to the unjustified fear of other people. Had we not used our media in such a way that vilified guns and instilled fear in Non-Gunners, Kent and I *could have* put our guns on the table. All I wanted to do was share my new SIG with a friend. But I couldn't. Not only were laws preventing me from laying my pistol on the table, I was also concerned with scaring people even though I know the fear to be unjustified. Concealment in public is something carriers are fully aware of and work very hard to perfect although it can at times be very burdensome. We buy many different holsters, special clothing, dress around our gun, stay aware of buildings we can and cannot enter and keep up to date on State to State travel laws, among many other hoops we jump through on a daily basis. For what reason? To not scare people? To not risk some fearful person calling the cops at the mere sight of a "good gun?"

So the conversation with Kent started out as a laugh at the ignorance we have created in our society, but brought up some serious social issues. We realized that we go to great lengths to accommodate people who don't understand guns and we take their concerns into careful consideration every day. Although we don't feel we should have to, it has become part of our culture.

Now to those reading this and saying, "Concealment is for the purpose of deterring crime by not letting the Bad Guys know there are guns in public," I understand that perspective but will include the fact that while this may be true, unjustified fear of guns has also become a major bi-product of this policy coupled with misleading media narrative.

I often get asked by Anti-Gunners if I'm carrying. The question is not asked in a casual way and it's not asked in my best interest. It's asked with intensity like no other question. When they ask, "Are you carrying right now?" they ask with a curious fascination and excitement because they realize that in this very moment they are about to find out if there is a loaded gun in their presence. This has huge meaning to some Anti-Gunners because the excitement they have built up around the topic is electric. They don't ask that question like they would ask you where you got your suit. They ask it with great anticipation, anxiety and even fear of the answer they will get. They want to know because they are genuinely curious, but to them this is the most taboo of all topics; "a real loaded gun."

Nelson Noguns: Do you have a gun on you right now?

Pat Riot: Does it matter?

Nelson Noguns: Well, uh, no, I mean, I was just wondering.

Pat Riot: Wondering about what?

Nelson Noguns: I'd just like to know who has a gun and who doesn't.

Pat Riot: So would you prefer open carry? That way you would know.

Nelson Noguns: No way! Then we would have the Wild West.

Pat Riot: What do you mean, the Wild West?

Nelson Noguns: Everyone running around with guns, are you kidding me? No thanks! I don't need to get caught in the middle of a gun fight every time I go to the grocery store.

Pat Riot: So, because you can see a gun, it somehow makes people act irresponsibly?

Nelson Noguns: Look, people don't need to be out in public with their guns on their hip. It's too dangerous.

Pat Riot: So you prefer I keep it my little secret?

Nelson Noguns: No. I just think I'm entitled to know who has a gun and who doesn't.

Pat Riot: You're entitled? So let me get this straight, you don't like open carry, but you want to know who has a gun on them?

Nelson Noguns: Well...um, not exactly.

Pat Riot: You don't know what you want, do you? That's ok. Listen.....
Come over here.... Be quiet though....
<look to the left, then to the right suspiciously>
You ready?

Nelson Noguns: Yeah, yeah, OK.

Pat Riot: Shhhh... Here it is. Don't touch it. That's a Smith and Wetson X924 Magnet double dumper with a reverse coil barrel and a sling-shot relay. What do you think of that?

Good Gun Bad Guy

Nelson Noguns: Whoa....Is it loaded?

Pat Riot: Of course it's loaded you knucklehead. What good would it be if it wasn't?

Don't forget, many Anti-Gunners have no, or at best, very limited experience with guns yet they talk a lot about how bad they are. Some of them have been media-manipulated to the point they will have visceral reactions to the word gun.

The fear and animosity many have built up around guns is intense to them, yet they most often have no real experience with firearms. Murder is the typical "go to" vision an Anti-Gunner will associate with guns whereas a Pro-Gunner wants to know about sights, barrel length, trigger take-up and any number of other functionality related topics. When such a pent-up curiosity is created around something with no outlet to satisfy that curiosity, an obsessive attitude can start to form. In many ways this can be resolved simply and easily, but often Anti-Gunners put themselves in a position where they make accessibility to guns impossible for themselves because they have denounced them in such a way that showing any interest, even just for educational purposes, would seem hypocritical and counter-productive to their cause. In other words, they might lose credibility in their anti-gun circles if they were seen at the range. I've seen the backlash Anti-Gunners get on social media from their fellow Anti-Gunners, even when they are simply gathering experiential data for the purposes of bolstering their cause. They will eat their own rather than risk losing them to the other side.

Carry laws differ dramatically from State to State. Some States have extremely restrictive laws, while some have no restrictions at all.

Alaska, Arizona, Arkansas, Kansas, Maine and Vermont have "Constitutional Carry," which means a resident can carry without the requirement of a government issued license. However, if a convicted felon is caught carrying in those States, the penalties are stiff. Of the States that do require a license to carry, a common requirement is the absence of any felony convictions. In other words, you must first have a clean record before getting approved for a carry license. These two carry philosophies seem to have the same end result. Without getting into the specific requirements of each state; in basic terms, if you have a felony you can't carry and if you don't, you can. The difference is in how the "non-license States" have a penalty if you already are a felon and are caught carrying, while the "license States" turn you into a felon if you carry without a license even if you have never committed a crime in your life. The freedom is put in the hands of the citizens in the "non-license States," while leverage is used on the citizens in the "license States." Wouldn't the end result be the same without the requirement of a carry license? The difference between the two is that in the "non-license States" law enforcement is focused on the Bad Guys carrying guns, while in the "license States" the restrictions are placed on everyone whether criminal or not. The majority of States without carry license requirements fall within the average to lowest crime rates with Maine and Vermont being the two lowest in the country.

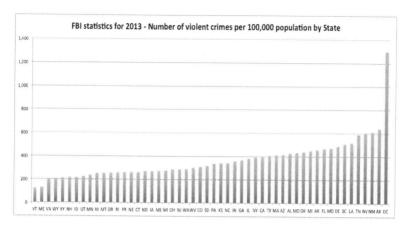

FBI statistics for 2013 - Number of violent crimes per 100,000 population by State

Donald Trump handled an NBC reporter perfectly when he was asked about if he was carrying a gun. He responded simply by saying, "It's none of your business." This response was perfect because the reporter was most likely trying to serve two purposes by invading Mr. Trump's privacy. She was trying to expose him in some childish way and satisfy her own curiosity. His answer didn't allow her any satisfaction.

Of course Anti-Gunners will deny the curiosity factor and many may truly be in denial that Pro-2nd Amendment advocates walk loaded among them but the struggle between knowing and not knowing is real. A woman I know once told me, "I don't want the guy in line next to me at the coffee shop to have a gun on him." I asked her why and she said she was afraid he might pull it out and start killing people. This mentality represents the sad truth that the media has corrupted the minds of people. If the anti-gun rhetoric and imagery were to stop for any length of time, this type of fear in people would start to dissipate and they would go about their lives in a normal healthy way; maybe even stop fearing guns, but it's the mission of the Anti-2nd Radicals to continue to perpetuate the fear. The fear of guns is something that must continue to be fueled or it will die. If people were no longer afraid of guns, who would vote for the anti-gun politicians? It would be nice if everyone could think logically but human nature shows us that some cannot. Fear has been successfully intertwined into the gun conversation. It is the fuel that pushes the argument.

If gun activity in this country didn't change at all but the fear of guns was reduced through education and accurate media representation, the argument for gun-control would lose its strength. In other words, if people suddenly were no longer afraid of guns everything would change. Imagine if the media injected the fear of driving into the conversation every time the topic of cars came up. Remember, more people die in their cars than do with guns. So, what if every time there was a car accident involving 3 or more people (mass car killing), the President got on TV and pleaded with the people to support him in his next illegal action against auto manufactures? Imagine him saying, "We will not stand for this senseless loss of life any longer. We must, once and for all, put a stop to car deaths." Our society does the exact opposite. Not only do we make it a point to try and *not* scare people about automobile travel, we actually advertise the sale of cars on TV. That's right, we promote these deadly things and even encourage the use of them. I know. crazy, right? Don't get me wrong. I love cars. I'm a collector. I'm just trying to make a point here. It's actually very rarely the fault of the car, rather the fault of the driver when an accident occurs. Of course we see the logic here because we all know that people can drive irresponsibly, text while driving, drive drunk or any number of things and we never ever blame the car. Heck, any sixteen year old can get his hands on a car. The fear that surrounds guns is perpetrated for a reason but many people are becoming wise to the misleading nature of the anti-gun narrative.

My experience with new gun owners has always been the same. At first they are hesitant and even scared of the gun but that fear quickly changes. Once they become familiar and gain knowledge on the topic, the fear turns into confidence and a real sense of enjoyment. I wanted to get some insight on that exact topic from someone who works with new gun owners on a regular basis. Public perception of guns is often distorted to make the average non-gun owner very fearful of guns so it is always a good idea to refer to the Pros for honest accurate information. Leo Nicotera is an NRA firearms Instructor and co-owner of Training House Saratoga.

DW: Hi Leo, Thanks so much for taking the time to answer a few questions.

LN: Anytime. I'm happy to do it.

DW: What would you say to the accusation that guns are dangerous and used to kill people?

LN: A gun is a tool that can be used for many purposes, no different than a spoon or a knife. I have spoons in my house and I haven't made myself fat with them, nor have I harmed anyone else with them. I have knives I haven't stabbed anyone with, and I have guns, which I haven't shot anyone with. Growing up I had rifles and shotguns in one corner of my room and the ammo for them on a bookshelf in the other. It never occurred to me to put the two together to hurt anyone. A tool isn't dangerous, it's the morals of the person holding it that need the attention.

DW: Are there any psychological challenges a person goes through when they begin carrying?

LN: The first time you carry your firearm on your person for self-defense, it's like carrying a big red brick. At least that's the way that it feels. It takes a long time, carrying that, before it's as comfortable as carrying your keys with you. Carrying for the first time should be the most mellowing force you experience in your life as it comes with great responsibility.

DW: What are some responses you get from people after their first day at the range?

LN: We get some really great comments and expressions from people! Typically they start out the day out a little timid, as most people do with anything new. But by the end of the day, they've got this huge smile on their face that goes along with the "Wow. I really had a good time!" That first day takes away the mystery of the firearm and turns it into a truly fun experience they enjoyed. They had a great time!

DW: As we see the number of new gun owners rise very quickly in America, it seems to be clear that people are catching on to exactly what you are saying. Thanks so much!

Good Gun Bad Guy

2. FALSE NARRATIVE

The good guy had a gun and the bad guy didn't. What happened?

The bad guy had a gun and the good guy didn't. What happened?

I heard a news broadcast recently and a question was asked that really helped me see how easy it is for the media to mislead their viewers. When people don't have an educated view with respect to a given topic and the media is there to implement a perspective for them, the results typically end up with the viewer accepting the premise that they are given.

Let's look at the misleading question and explore the power it has to anchor a belief into the minds of unsuspecting viewers. This question is loaded and we are fed this type of brainwashing on a daily basis. Here's the question:

"Since guns are dangerous, do you think restrictions are necessary?"

Now, on the surface this question may look harmless but it's implications are very destructive. As soon as that question is asked, millions of viewers are screaming at their TVs saying: "Yes! Absolutely! Restrict all gun ownership!" Many are also watching while shaking their head in frustration because we know that something is wrong here, but maybe we can't quite put our finger on it. Let's put our finger on it now.

First we will look at the "Since guns are dangerous" portion of the sentence. This implies that it has already been determined as fact that guns are dangerous. The word "Since" implies that there is no question about the rest of the statement. This does not leave the viewer the opportunity to even question the accusation that guns are dangerous. The determination has been made for you by using the word "since." Look at the first half of the question again. It's very misleading. A more honest and thought provoking way to present this would be to ask the viewer *if* they think guns are dangerous. That way you could decide for yourself but even then there is an inherent association with the words "guns" and "dangerous". Instead of letting you decide for yourself if guns are dangerous, they have already made that determination for you. Even if you were able to catch the implication, you wouldn't have time to evaluate it because it is followed up with a question. Why is it a problem to follow up that accusation with a question you may ask?

The second part of the question is the trickiest of all. When a question is asked, our brains instantly go to work at trying to answer the question. That's just how it goes. Our brains are problem-solving machines and they don't always stop to validate whether or not the question is based in truth. Because our brains instantly go to work at answering the question we don't always consider the misleading nature of the question itself.

Have you ever had a dream that was so abstract it made absolutely no sense when you woke up? This is an example of your brain trying to solve a problem without you consciously knowing about it. In other words, your brain will automatically go to work on a problem for you in order to answer a question. In the case of a dream it may be a question you are trying to resolve from the day before.

So anytime you are asked a question your brain jumps into

action. Marketers and media outlets know this tactic and use it on you every single day. You may remember the Burger King slogan: "Aren't you hungry for Burger King now?" from the 90s. Look it up. It's a simple yet brilliant way to distract you from any fact-finding or anything else that may be going on in your life and get you to decide if you are hungry for Burger King while looking at juicy, delicious burgers on the grill. Try watching that commercial and not want a Whopper. Heck, you probably want one right now. I talk more about this topic in the chapter "Have you been brainwashed?" in my book Defining Success in America.

Back to the question at hand: *"Since guns are dangerous, do you think restrictions are necessary?"*

Before you have a chance to evaluate for yourself whether or not "guns are dangerous", your brain is hard at work to make a determination on if you think restrictions are necessary. Your brain already assumes guns are dangerous so of course you would think restrictions are necessary. How many people do you think fall for this on a daily basis? These people are voters. It's time to step up the game and make sure that the Anti-2nd Radicals know that we are on to the misleading rhetoric and falsehoods they propagate. Here's a way to flip the question and get people thinking.

"Because guns save lives, do you think restricting them limits the ability of people to protect themselves in times of danger?"

Stated this way, we would respond by saying: "Of course it does!" In this question, we assume that guns save lives and we help people see the danger of restricting them. I like this question a whole lot better. It frames the topic in a proactive way because studies have shown that guns save lives 60 times more than they take them. In other words, how does it help me if something I need is restricted? The answer of course is: "It doesn't." It can be compared to the following question:

"Because gasoline is necessary to operate most vehicles, is it ok to restrict some people from purchasing it?"

The media has been misleading people about guns for a long time. This is nothing new. Here are a couple pieces of misleading propaganda spewed from two very influential media outlets. Let's break them down and explore the power they have in misguiding people and redirecting the narrative & public opinion as it relates to guns.

"We will never fully solve our nation's horrific problem of gun violence unless we ban the manufacture and sale of handguns and semi-automatic assault weapons." --USA Today, December 29, 1993

If it's true that most people believe everything they read, then this quote wins the prize for effectively tarnishing the gun culture and manipulating the minds of the people. Notice the key words in this one. "Horrific", "Gun Violence", "Ban", "Handguns", Assault Weapons". Masterfully written, this misleads in a way that people would most often not even recognize.

Take the first part: *"We will never solve."* This is to generate a feeling of hopelessness in the minds of the readers. "If we can never solve it, that would be terrible."

Next they present the idea that there is a "Horrific" problem and it is "Nationwide". The reader is inclined to put the two together and become fearful. *"Oh my God, we're in trouble!"*

Then they give you the misrepresentation that violence is caused by guns when they link the two words "Gun" and "Violence." Guns are not violent in the real world. People are. But that doesn't matter. If they can make guns violent in your mind, the job is complete.

They are just trying to create a narrative and want you to pay no attention to logic.

Now at this point the reader is scared, feeling ineffective and placing the blame on guns. Let's summarize up to that point. *"We will never fully solve our nation's horrific problem of gun violence."* I don't know about you but it sounds pretty hopeless to me.

But wait there's more! The writer then adds the very important word: "Unless." This is a tactic that is used in those infamous "As seen on TV" ads where they create the problem for you, then give you the solution. At this point the reader is saying *"What?! Anything! I'll do anything to stop this horrific gun violence. What is it? Just tell me damn it!"*

Then they give you the solution to the problem they fabricated. Here's the answer to the problem. Are you ready? All we have to do to solve this horrific problem of gun violence is: *"Ban the manufacture and sale of handguns and semi-automatic assault weapons."* Easy. Problem solved.

The reader says in their mind: *"Fine. Let's do it, whatever it takes."* And the news outlet is hopeful to add a new addition or two to their anti-gun family of robotic reactively-programmed minions. That's what they do. They have been doing it forever and they are very good at it. They are so good that it goes unrecognized most of the time and is still very effective. It's all right there in one masterfully crafted sentence. Read the entire sentence again but this time when you read it try to imagine what it would be like for someone who was on the fence about guns.

"We will never fully solve our nation's horrific problem of gun violence unless we ban the manufacture and sale of handguns and semi-automatic assault weapons."

If Americans don't realize soon how manipulative some media outlets can be, we will eventually live among a society of people who buy clothing based on trends, drive cars we believe will save the planet and eat cereal because it has a cute cartoon character on the box and claims to be "packed with wholesome goodness." Thank God that hasn't happened. What is "wholesome goodness" anyway?

Here's another powerful and misleading newspaper quote. This one does not hold back. It's blatant attempt at manipulating the thought process of its readers is right out in the open.

"Why should America adopt a policy of near-zero tolerance for private gun ownership? Who can still argue compellingly that Americans can be trusted to handle guns safely? We think the time has come for Americans to tell the truth about guns. They are not for us, we cannot handle them." --Los Angeles Times, December 28, 1993

This one is loaded with misleading rhetoric. Look at the first sentence carefully.

"Why should America adopt a policy of near-zero tolerance for private gun ownership?"

"Why should" presupposes that we "should". This misleading piece gets the brain searching for an answer to why we should rather than ask the reader if they think a policy should even be adopted at all. Very clever.

"Who can still argue compellingly that Americans can be trusted to handle guns safely?"

This sentence implies that there is no compelling argument at all. That we are incapable of being trusted. Once trust is lost, it is very hard to get back. This sentence obliterates trust with nothing to support the claim. It also implies that we (including the reader) need someone (Government) to hold our hand and make sure we don't hurt ourselves or others. This sentence appeals to the fearful ones. If you are already scared of guns and you know that you can't handle them, this sentence reinforces your fear and implies that most others are also firearm-challenged. At the same time, it enrages the independent thinkers and the self-sufficient responsible people.

"We think the time has come for Americans to tell the truth about guns."

The "We think" part implies the majority group is in favor. In other words, if you disagree, you are the opposition. This sentence also implies that Americans are liars, and nobody likes a liar. So whose side are you on; the majority of truth seekers or the degenerate group of liars? Who the heck is "we" anyway? Is it ok for some writer at the LA Times to make these determinations?

"They are not for us, we cannot handle them."

Again, this implies that the majority has already decided and it's now just a matter of the reader jumping on board. My question is, who decided they're not for us...some fearful liberal newspaper writer? As for the "we cannot handle them" piece... Speak for yourself!

Terminology is another way Anti-Gunners misrepresent guns and manipulate the narrative. Many Pro-Gunners have a problem with the terminology used against guns and gun owners because we know it is misleading. The idea that internal representations can be altered by words may sound impossible at first, and if you point out an instance when you think words were used to do damage you may be labeled a conspiracy theorist but words in fact are a very powerful tool in the war against guns because they change the internal representation and ultimately the thought process of people. I'm not talking about words affecting our emotions, I'm referring to the mental imagery words create. Anti-Gunners will typically insert nomenclatures and talking points into the conversation for the purpose of influencing the internal representation of anyone listening. It's powerful because our minds easily accept this type of influence. If the thought process is not influenced quickly, repetitive reinforcement will ultimately do the trick.

Just like McDonalds convinces you you're "lovin it" and Nike encourages you to "just do it," the anti-gun lobby has taught you that guns "assault" or are "violent." This is accomplished by injecting terms like "Assault Weapon" and "Gun Violence" into the conversation. These and other terms are relentlessly and unapologetically pounded into the narrative until they become a common belief. Of course we know logically that guns are not violent and they do not assault, rather people do. These marketing strategies are as basic as they come. Repetition and making the topic a common part of the conversation perpetuate the notion of truth and solidify the belief in the minds of people. The American social construct is different than many Countries, so where forceful dictatorship strategies can't be used, a more friendly, non-invasive strategy helps sway people to support a cause or welcome a new belief.

NBA coaches have been known to teach their players this fundamental strategy for the purpose of winning games. The habit of seeing the ball go through the hoop before taking the shot is something that has been proven to bring real results. "Seeing it and believing it before you achieve it" is a way to set your mind up to take ownership of the future desired outcome and ultimately act with confidence and a higher level of effectiveness. Once you own it, it becomes a reality in your brain which allows you to take action with confidence and the repetitive reinforcement makes it believable to you. After achieving the result you begin to develop a strong belief that you have the capability and the momentum builds upon itself. It becomes a belief in the mind of the basketball player, without a doubt, that he can make the shot. It also becomes a belief in the minds of people that guns are violent.

If I told you smoking cigarettes will make you sophisticated you would probably think I was crazy. But if I told you every single day and you started seeing billboards displaying sophisticated looking people smoking, you might start to think about it. If every time you saw an advertisement about cigarettes, the people in them looked "sophisticated," you may begin to accept the notion. If the image of sophistication were attached to cigarettes on a consistent basis with full media support, propagated in a way that seemed popular to everyone it may even start to become public opinion that cigarettes are in fact a viable way to become (or at least appear to be) sophisticated. Nonsense right? Not so fast. That is exactly what happened in the 1920's after World War I. Cigarettes became sophisticated and even glamorous. Eventually the narrative would be manipulated again to bend public opinion into believing that cigarettes were cool. There was even a brand of cigarettes named "Kool." Never mind the health risks, image was much more important and people took the bait, hook, line and sinker.

The same thing has been done in recent years with respect to the internal representation people have of guns. Many different terms have been injected into the conversation for the purpose of arousing negative or fearful thoughts when the topic of guns is brought up. Pro-Gunners even tend to use the terminology without realizing it or recognizing the negative affects it has on the overall cultural narrative.

I have collected a few terms that I'm sure you have heard but may not have recognized their impact and the intent behind their usage.

- **Assault Rifle** – This term was inserted into the conversation in the 1990s for the purpose of demonizing military styled rifles while creating fear and anger among society. That fear and anger would eventually be used to rally Anti-Gunners and encourage them to support bans against the rifles. A group of anti-gun Democratic politicians would eventually determine what defined an "Assault Rifle" and the term would be injected into the conversation for political purposes in the war on guns. There was no such thing as an "Assault Rifle" in our American culture until anti-gun politicians created it. They even tried justifying the term by misleading the public to believe that the "AR" in AR-15 stood for "Assault Rifle" when in fact it stands for "Armalite Rifle" after the company that created it.

- **Common Sense Gun Safety** – is a term used to gain the support of people when it comes time to support gun restrictions. The term "Common Sense" is used to gain leverage over people because if you don't support common sense you must be nonsensical and no one would want to be labeled nonsensical. "Gun Safety" implies that guns are not safe and the implication is that we must do something to change that. This just promotes fear and furthers the false narrative that guns are dangerous while influencing people to jump on the anti-gun bandwagon.

- **Gun Violence** – is a term designed to associate fear with guns. Guns are not violent. People are violent, but focusing on the violent tendencies in people does not help further the war on guns. The Anti-2nd Amendment Radicals understand that in order to increase the fear and anger in people they must brainwash them to believe that violence is caused by guns. This term works like magic. If the Anti-2nd Radicals were honest they would use the term "Violent Behavior" and keep the "Gun" out of it because without the behavior of the human involved, the gun would just sit there. However, without the gun involved the human would use something else. Attaching the word "violence" to the word "gun" as often as possible influences people to associated the two as synonyms.

- **Gun Control** – is an interesting term because it implies a few things. The first and most misleading implication is the idea that a gun would need to be controlled, as if it had a mind of it's own. This is yet another way of putting the focus on the gun and taking it off the human behavior. It sets the gun up to appear to be the thing that needs to be "controlled." It is another way word association is used. Another misleading implication is that controlling the illegal or violent use of guns is actually possible. It simply is not. Removing guns from the hands of Bad Guys will never happen. To imply that it could and getting people to believe it is possible is just another recruitment tactic used by anti-gun politicians. The truth is, you cannot control illegal gun use through legislation. The simple fact is that criminals do not follow laws. That's inherent in their nature; so how is it that laws would have any impact on their behavior? Law-abiding citizens however, *are* affected by laws but the Good Guys are certainly not the ones politicians are trying to control….right? It would only make logical sense that if you wanted to control law-abiding citizen, you would use laws to do it. So you may ask: Who is "Gun Control" intended to affect?

- **High powered** – The term "High Powered" can be attached to anything to give it a little more punch. When it comes to guns, the term "High Powered" is supposed to make you think they are more deadly. Better watch out for those "High Powered" guns as opposed to the average powered guns or the low powered guns. It's just added for effect and to create more fear.

- **High Capacity** – is used to vilify magazines or as Anti-Gunners call them – "clips." By using the term "High Capacity" you are encouraged to think they are a specially designed device used for taking more lives. "capacity" refers to the amount of cartridges a magazine or feeding device can hold. Put the word "High" in front of it and now people are supposed to think they are dealing with a crazy killing machine.

- **Wild West** – is a term used in the war on guns to create an image of uncontrollable gun-fights in public. The idea behind this is to make you think that if guns are carried in public, people will forget how to control themselves and they will begin to act uncivilized. This term is also used to create a visual image of over-testosterone men acting out to show everyone how "manly" they are. The intent is to bolster the belief that constant gun-fights will break out in the streets. The hope is that you will also believe that everyone will have guns and they will be killing each other for the most trivial of issues – like cutting off in traffic or stealing parking spots. They want you to believe that no one will be safe leaving their home because once people are in possession of a gun they act irrationally. The "Wild West" term brings with it a vivid visual component and is used to create fear.

- **"We need to have the conversation so we can find a solution to gun violence."** – is not term but a common statement used by a group that gets their information from an anti-gun media. They really don't want to have a conversation about anything. This statement is designed to change the narrative. This statement suggests that the pro-gun community is being unreasonable by not discussing issues of violence while making the Anti-Gunners appear noble and concerned about the welfare of everyone. It also implies that we have not found solutions to the problem of violent felons acquiring guns. This statement screams, *"I have no idea what laws are on the books and not being enforced. I am only repeating what I heard last night on Network news."* The truth is, all the laws we need to solve the problem of mentally incapacitated people and violent criminals acquiring firearms are in place. The problem is, they are not enforced. The records of mentally incompetent people are not added to the National Instant Check System, so many people who shouldn't own firearms are able to purchase them legally. Killers are able to purchase guns because politicians refuse to put the necessary data in the system. *"38 States submit less than 80 percent of their felony convictions to the system. Leaving more than 7,000,000 felony convictions in the dark." In 2010 roughly 80,000 prohibited people committed a felony by trying to buy a gun. Just 44 were prosecuted for it." – Wayne LaPierre, NRA CEO.* What happens next is routine. Violence occurs, guns are blamed, and again anti-gun politicians demand something be done. The rally cries begin, "the desperate need to find a solution" becomes the narrative and more laws are introduced. Politicians pursue the expansion of a broken system but do nothing to fix it and continue to claim that we need to find a solution.

These are just a few of the misleading terms being used by people who know nothing about guns and are driven by an anti-gun agenda and led by an anti-gun media. They spread their message through any and every medium available with the intent of misleading the public and instilling fear under the guise of educating them. If you really wanted to learn about something wouldn't you seek out the knowledge of experts? You wouldn't ask a heroin dealer to teach you about organic foods, or a preschooler to teach you calculus, would you? So why would you take the advice or entertain the opinions of an Anti-Gunner over someone who has knowledge of and a healthy respect for guns? Instead of getting information from the Pros, they take it from the Pundits.

A big part of the war on guns is the way us Pro-Gunners have been put in a position of reactive, defensive response. It seems we are always defending our rights rather than exercising them. It's time to turn the tables and take a proactive approach. The perspective of questions and terms like these and their implications are what influence public opinion. The angle people use to change the perspective of others is crucial in this battle to preserve our rights and safety. It's time to recognize their tactics. You wouldn't expect to win a game if you didn't know the rules. The problem is there is no rule book available and the people hosting this game of lies wouldn't share their tactics with you anyway.

One goal within their twisted game is to demonize the act of protecting yourself. Their job is to make you look (and feel) like a complete nutcase for carrying a gun around in public. They do it by positioning you as an outcast. It's one thing to convince people that their current way of doing something is bad when trying to sell them cleaning supplies, but it's a completely different thing when you try to convince people that defending themselves is a bad thing. The media convinces people of this every day and it would seem the Anti-2nd Radicals have made this their mission. The sad fact is that many people involved in tragic, violent attacks are often of the anti-gun mindset and have taught themselves (or allowed themselves to be taught) to denounce guns. So, at the time when a gun could have saved their life or a loved-one's life, they rendered themselves unarmed and helpless just so they could fall in line with the anti-gun beliefs they have been programmed to support. Some paid dearly for holding strong to their belief.

It's not so bad that the Anti-Gunners will *tell* you that having guns to protect yourself is unsafe, but that they actually *believe* it, is a much scarier thought. This simply means that people are easily misled. In America today, we need to take the idea of self-defense very seriously. How is it that smart, well-intended people can look reality in the face yet believe a media narrative that tells them the exact opposite? What is it that causes people to deny reality?

The answer is – Fear; fear of guns and fear of being an outcast.

To some people, guns are the most terrifying things, even more than driving cars. Which, by the way will kill more people this year than guns.

The New York Times (in an attempt to make gun deaths look more numerous than auto related deaths) published an article in 2014 that stated data from the "Violence Policy Center" confirmed a report that gun related deaths exceeded auto related deaths in 2011. Read further and you learn that, yes indeed gun related deaths exceeded auto related deaths in 14 states. Well, I'm no math scholar but given the fact that there are 50 states, my logic tells me that more people still die in their cars. Why are we not terrifying people with car death statistics and why would they put a piece of misleading data like that out to the public? Because it works. Most people don't consider the fact that 36 states have fewer gun deaths than car deaths because the narrative is presented in a way that only highlights what they want you to focus on. In this case giving the reader only certain information creates a vision and influences their internal representation in the exact way they want.

Anti-2nd Radicals and the media would like everyone to believe that guns are constantly in the hands of babies. They want the world to think that children are accidentally killing each other every day with loaded guns that are just lying around the house. They hope to convince you that without more gun laws, we would have the wild west where people are having showdowns in the streets. They would like you to envision gun fights breaking out every time someone bumps into another person's shopping cart in the produce section. They would also love for you to believe that guns make people behave dangerously and irresponsibly.

In late February, 2016 the Houston Chronicle published an article that, at first glance, appeared to be about the anger of college professors. The professors were angry that they were being silenced in their own classrooms, all due to a new on-campus carry law for Universities that would go into affect in the upcoming month of August. Since the new state law would allow students to carry firearms on campus for the purpose of self-protection, the staff were specifically told by the University of Houston Faculty Senate to not engage in any communication that may anger students who carried guns. There was even an instructional slide show presentation to alert the professors and staff of the seriousness of the matter. The slide show and instructions expressed the potential dangers of getting into any type of disagreement or debate with a student, indicating that the outcome could be deadly. Some of the things that were specifically noted and suggested to faculty were:

- *Be careful discussing sensitive topics*
- *Drop certain topics from your curriculum*
- *Don't "go there" if you sense anger*
- *Limit student access off hours*

They are told, that as soon as guns are brought into the picture they should be very careful how they interact with those people who could be carrying. Jonathan Snow, President of the Senate said, *"The faculty are increasingly unhappy with the law. "I've been screamed at. I've been accused of complicity. It's been kind of rough."* Snow also said, *"Academics know the intrusion of gun culture into campus inevitably harms academic culture."*

Now lets break this down, cut through the rhetoric and diffuse the hysterics. On the surface, this implementation of the narrative depicting professors as victims who are being silenced against their will is not surprising. What else would you expect from anti-gun liberals? Even six months before the new policy even went into effect they are jumping on the victim bandwagon while creating the image of gun owners as irrational maniacs. The idea that the anti-gun crowd would create this victim-hood not only plays into their wheelhouse but also helps perpetuate the narrative that gun owners are angry, dangerous and will just as soon kill you if you look at them sideways. Pushing this idea is very helpful to their agenda and it plays right into the fears and anger of all the other Anti-2nd Radicals with the hopes of radicalizing as many more new Anti-Gunners as possible.

When I first read about this, I didn't recognize the fact that liberal policies are starting to come back to bite the ones who implement them. In this case, we are looking at something similar to political correctness where it is unacceptable to say certain things for the fear of offending someone. In this situation the fear is "getting killed." It's a completely unjustified fear but it is interesting to watch them inflict it on themselves. Although gun owners and especially legal conceal carriers are some of the most respectful and responsible people I have ever met, it is quite refreshing to see corrupt, irrational liberal policies come back to haunt the perpetrators.

This is yet another case of not letting a good chance to push the anti-gun agenda go to waste. Snow's comment, *"Academics know the intrusion of gun culture into campus inevitably harms academic culture,"* is misleading but a great propaganda piece none the less. Statistics show that killers choose Gun Free Zones 69% of the time but facts like that don't support the case for fear-mongering Anti-2nd Amendment Radicals. My hypothesis is that this push to silence themselves will not go any further than this because these people will soon realize that they are falling victim to their own policies. I do however foresee them fabricating an incident in the future as a way of showing guns on campus being a bad idea. Maybe they stage a firearm mishap, shooting or simply talk of such that gets national attention but never has any substantial credibility. We'll see. It is always entertaining to watch their creative narratives play out.

Vermont had the lowest gun related crime rate in the country in 2010 *and* the most relaxed gun restrictions. In 2015 Maine jumped on board with a constitutional carry law similar to Alaska, Arizona, Arkansas, Kansas, and Vermont which respect the right of the people to carry a concealed firearm. They recognize the importance of concealed-carry and they see the great results that are achieved when citizens are able to arm themselves. To the contrary, Massachusetts passed a law restricting gun use in 1998 and the results have been the exact opposite. After Massachusetts' 1998 gun restrictions, gun ownership rates dropped but violent crimes and murders increased. The Anti-2nd Amendment Radicals won't tell you about that part.

The thought of the wild west and the imagery that the progressive left hopes to implant in your mind is of people having constant shootouts in the streets and showdowns at high noon. They want you to live in fear of uncontrolled rampant gun battles over trivial issues and they want you to believe they are inevitable if we don't implement strict gun control immediately on a national level. This is one of the favorite scenarios because it has such a vivid visual component. They want you to envision average Americans running around shooting each other. The truth is the states with the most relaxed gun restrictions enjoy the most peaceful, non-violent living conditions. The areas with the strictest gun control like the Cities of

Chicago and Washington D.C. are where the most violence occurs because there are no opposing "good guns" to keep the Bad Guys on their best behavior. So I suppose if there were anything close to the wild west in America it could be found in the highly gun-restricted Democrat-run areas. They don't want you to look at that, which is why you won't see the rampant gang violence, murders and black-on-black crime in any realistic proportion on the evening news. You will however see every coffee shop, church and school shooting because that fits the narrative that supports their mission. The mission is to make the violence appear to be right in your backyard and fill you with fear. Yes, you. The average middle-class American voter.

The Anti-2nd Radicals understand that imagery is the most important tool they have. They understand that by creating a visual scenario for you to download into your brain over and over again, they will get you to believe whatever they want. This is why I can say "I'm lovin' it" and you instantly think of McDonalds. It's because McDonald's marketing companies have ingrained that slogan and the images that go with it into your brain through repetition. The Anti-Gunners and Anti-2nd Amendment Radicals will continue to perpetrate scenarios that demonize guns and gun owners as long as they can. They will continue to implement visuals into your brain as often and with as much influence as they can because their mission is to make you believe that guns are bad and gun owners are irresponsible.

Another narrative-manipulating tactic that has been implemented during the Obama administration is the changing of the definition of "Mass Shooting." Many people don't even know how the media determines if something is a "Mass Shooting." But being able to use the term sure is a good way for the media to get the attention of average Americans at their dinner tables. Up until 2013 the FBI set the standard and definition of a "Mass Shooting" to be a single attack in which 4 or more victims were killed. In 2013 President

Obama changed the definition of "Mass Shooting" by mandate to a single attack in which 3 or more victims were killed. This may not seem like a big deal; but ask yourself why it would be so important to him to change the definition? Some people will argue that by lowering the threshold of "number of people" in a mass shooting from 4 to 3, it would make it easier to qualify more mass shootings for the purpose of media hype and gun-bashing.

The strongest human motivator is fear and the people who seek control understand this very well. They will use a false narrative to instill fear in the public.

In a 2015 public speech after the Roseburg, Oregon Community College shooting, President Obama said this:

"And what's become routine, of course, is the response of those who oppose any kind of commonsense gun legislation." "We'll need more guns they'll argue; fewer gun safety laws. Does anybody really believe that? There are scores of responsible gun owners in this country. They know that's not true."

This statement was crafted to create the narrative that there is a group of unsafe, unreasonable gun owners with no common sense out there and the majority of gun owners oppose them. This false narrative is concocted to create division within the pro-gun community. The creation of the "unreasonable," "unsafe" gun owners with "no common sense" is called a "straw man." This is an opponent that doesn't exist, but is created for the sake of the narrative and to give people a target to rally against. His attempt with this is to put Pro-Gunners against themselves by encouraging them to believe that some in their group are being unreasonable. The strategy is designed to get gun owners to turn on each other. This is a very tricky and well-crafted media tactic.

President Obama also said, *"This is something we should politicize."* *He then went on to try and turn gun owners against the NRA by saying, "I would particularly ask America's gun owners who are using those guns properly, safely, to hunt, for sport, for protecting their families to think about whether your views are properly being represented by the organization that suggests it's speaking for you."*

It would seem clear after reading between the lines that his motive is to demonize and divide gun owners for the sake of a political agenda. These talking points create the narrative and get picked up by network, cable and even local news. Many of these outlets don't mean any harm but they continue to pass along the latest misleading message from the White House.

The narrative of any story can be manipulated. It's all just a matter of which elements are focused on and which are deleted from the conversation. In the case of the first Fort Hood killing, the U.S. Government held on to the "workplace violence" narrative as long as they could to avoid calling the incident what it really was – an act of Islamic terrorism. It took two years and a lawsuit by family members and survivors to force the administration to change the classification to an "Act of Terrorism." Initially, reporters called it anything they could other than what it really was. Reporters, psychiatrists and even Senators were tripping over themselves to come up with other reasons for Hasan's deadly mission. Anything but the truth came out. They avoided the truth like the plague. They spread any number of false narratives to the public; from Hasan's psychological state being in question to anger because his superior didn't grant him a request. In 2013 FOX news finally released information calling the killer a "Soldier for Allah." Creating a false narrative is one of many strategies used in the war against the 2nd Amendment.

Good Gun Bad Guy

Have you ever noticed how Anti-2nd Radicals say things like *"We're not going to take away your guns"* when the topic of the 2nd Amendment comes up? This statement is loaded with reverse psychology. The statement: "We're not going to take away your guns" implies that they have the authority or ability to do so. This statement is designed to put the gun owner in a position of defense and subordination while it puts the gun-grabber in the position of authority and power. The idea behind this "gun-grab" is to make the gun owners feel and appear inferior, criminal, suspect and at the mercy of the gun-grabbers. The reality is exactly the opposite. The gun owners have the authority and the power because of the 2nd Amendment but the gun-grabbers have been strategic in setting up this particular positioning. They have been very careful about how they position themselves in the argument.

Anytime you tell someone that you are not going to do something to them, you're not going to take something from them, or you're not going to cause something to happen to them it assumes you have the authority and/or the ability to do so. That implied assumption is the effective component in this psychological game. The implication that they have the ability to "take away your guns" is a hidden message within the "gun-grab" argument. The hidden implication is that they have the authority and the ability to take your guns, but they're not going to do it. How nice of them. This strategy is designed to put the gun owner in a position of fear and causes them to take the defensive position in the argument.

When people are in a defensive position they get nothing done. At that point they are just trying to preserve what they have and are not focused on proactive forward movement. When a football team is on defense, their main objective is to prevent the offense from gaining ground. Sure they can get an interception but that is not their main priority. The gun-grabbers at the top pulling the strings of their minions are smarter than we make them out to be when it comes to positioning people. Many of the people we encounter on a day-to-day basis just follow the narrative that is given to them and may not realize the subtle nuances of the strategies that are being used to misguide them. They fall right into the game exactly where they are supposed to.

When someone tells you that you have nothing to worry about because they are not going to take away your guns, or ask you what you are so afraid of, they are trying to put you in a defensive position. That is how they are able to control the conversation and gain leverage over you. A typical response from pro-gunners when they are told, *"We're not going to take away your guns"* is: *"You're damn right you're not. I won't yet you!"* That's the exact position they want you in. They want you in a defensive mode and in a reactive state of mind. When people are in a defensive mode, they don't have the stability, power, leverage or confidence needed to win the argument. Similar to karate, when you are in a forward stance you are dangerous. When you are in a defensive position, you are protecting yourself. Pro-Gunners need to recognize this and start taking a forward stance. That is when progress will begin. That is how you control the narrative. We will eventually take control of the narrative but unfortunately it seems we must get pushed around quite a bit first. I am starting to see some forward movement from the Pro-Gunners but we are a long way from turning the argument around to the point we are teaching gun safety in our schools or advertising the latest handgun from Smith and Wesson on TV.

Gun-grabbers, Anti-Gunners and Liberal Democrats in general have been very successful in controlling the narrative around guns. Owning the narrative has been their saving grace because once the tables are turned and they are in the defensive position the game will be over; we then will have effectively taken the power of the argument away from them. My intent is to bring this to light so everyone understands what is happening psychologically. When we do, we will be able to put our effort into moving forward rather than spending our time and energy defending our rights. Forward movement may include things like: implementing retired veterans into our schools to protect our kids, putting the criminals on notice by letting them know we are armed and ready for them and banishing Gun Free Zones. Gun safety education in schools would also be a good forward moving step. By taking control of the gun narrative we can move the ball forward and bring back a healthy respect and appreciation of firearms. To do this we must first get through the psychological piece, put the Anti-2nd Amendment Radicals on notice and turn the tables. Anyone who advocates unarmed helplessness will then be on the defensive side of the argument.

On the surface, it would appear that the "gun grab" debate was just an argument to determine the validity of gun ownership. What is going on behind the debate is the important piece. We can argue and throw statistics at each other all day long but this book was written to put the focus on the thought-process behind the debate. It's about the idea that Anti-Gunners can put themselves and Pro-Gunners in the positions they want in order to manipulate the argument. This form of manipulation is brilliant because it is a hidden strategy that most people cannot see. You can't point your finger at the fact that one side is being manipulated through "defense positioning." It's just something that typically goes unnoticed. People don't recognize it so no one points it out but it is a perfect strategy.

The people who implement this defense positioning understand this and they know it is working to skew the narrative and convince the gun owners that they should be very fearful of losing their rights. The gun-grabbers create a strategy that puts them in control of the argument and they do it in a way that no one can accuse them of anything. Most of the anti-gun minions who participate in this rhetoric don't even recognize that they are using this defense

72

positioning strategy, but they do know that they have found a side that they feel safe on. Most don't understand that they, too, are being manipulated as warriors in this war on guns. It's my goal to put all the cards on the table and expose the strategies so we all have the same tools.

The strategies are brilliant and used every single day in many different "news" outlets. A perfect example of blind rhetoric with a complete disregard for logic is the statement made by MSNBC host Melissa Harris-Perry on January 2nd 2016. Perry is known for her progressive, left wing, anti-gun stance and really lets it shine in this one as she once again shows us the ignorance and lack of foresight the entire anti-gun media parade is built on.

In an attempt to justify gun confiscation Perry said, *"A lot of people shoot their wives with perfectly legal guns. They wouldn't if they did not have them."* This again, goes right to the idea that facts don't matter but narrative is king when it comes to Anti-2nd Amendment Radicals influencing the internal representation of people. In this case Perry is speaking to wives and letting every married woman across America know that, *yes, you too could possibly be shot and killed by your own husband. So you'd better support any and all gun restrictions we come up with. It's for your own good.* Remember, the mentality behind gun grabbing is fear based in a non-reality that guns cause people to act irresponsibly. So this statement by Perry is perfect because it speaks to the woman who doesn't know much about guns, sees her husband's guns and always wonders if having them in the house is a bad idea.

After listening to this fearful progressive rally cry by Perry, I thought it would be interesting to see just how thick they frost cake on this one. The first thing that became glaringly apparent to me is how Anti-2nd Radical groups and some left-wing media have this little niche of the anti-gun internet locked up. The correlation between domestic violence, military style firearms and a lack of mental health issues seem to be their sweet spot. They create a spin by using the new "Obama mandated mass shooting" term, which has been lowered to 3 from 4 people killed in any one incident, attach it to those scary black rifles they love to call "Assault Rifles" and fuse them together with the term "Domestic Violence".

This beautiful potpourri comes alive when they attach disclosures stating that no evidence of mental instability was ever brought to the attention of authorities. This allows for the viewer to eliminate mental instability as a valid cause of these incidents and focus on the gun as the culprit. I have to admit there are some very smart people out there packaging hand-picked data in a way that creates a convincing narrative. They are working 24-7 and doing some articulate number crunching and word-smithing to manipulate the way you think about guns. The media spinners (not surprisingly) include but are not limited to the following outlets: Huffington Post, MSNBC, Mayors against Illegal Guns and Everytown for Gun Safety.

Let's set some of their rhetoric straight. The reality is that the term "Domestic Violence" can qualify any boyfriend, girlfriend, husband, wife, ex-husband, ex-wife, ex-boyfriend, ex-girlfriend, female gay partner, male gay partner, roommate, brother, sister, mother, father, aunt, uncle, grandparent and so on. In other words, anyone to whom the shooter is closely related or living with can fall under the "Domestic Violence" category. The magic is in the way the data-spinners imply the "Helpless Wife" to be the only one used in collecting the data.

Next is of course the military style rifle or as the anti-gun crowd likes to deviously call them, "assault rifles" (because it supports their narrative). This is basically a modern day sporting rifle with one or more specific attachments that make it look scary. Oh yeah, most of

74

them are black too. I guess once you remove any wood grain from the rifle it makes it more dangerous. The most commonly purchased model among hunters and shooters is the AR-15. The Anti-2nd Radicals love to insert these rifles into the conversation any chance they get and they sometimes slip in the term "automatic" even when they know they are "semi-automatic." Hillary Clinton continues to use the term "automatic" for effect even when she knows the difference. Here is an exact quote from June 17th, 2014:

"First of all, I think as a teacher or really any parent, what's been happening with these school shootings should cause everybody to just think hard. We make hard choices and we balance competing values all the time. And I was disappointed that the Congress did not pass universal background checks after the horrors of the shootings at Sandy Hook, and now we've had more in the time since. And I don't think any parent—any person—should have to fear about their child going to school or going to college because someone, for whatever reason—psychological, emotional, political, [ideological], whatever it means—could possibly enter that school property with an automatic weapon and murder innocent children, students, teachers."

She used the term again in one of her CNN debates against Bernie Sanders while running in the 2016 elections. In fact there have been a number of times she has used it. You might ask yourself, "Does she not know the difference between automatic and semi-automatic?" I would venture to say that over the years, and being such an anti-gun advocate, someone has informed her of the difference. This is purely a tactic to further demonize guns and build more political weight against the 2nd Amendment. Every little bit helps.

Out of respect to the creativity of Anti-Gunners everywhere, I propose a new name for these rifles that is sure to keep Spin City feeling like they still have a seat at the big kid's table while also giving them ownership to terminology they can be proud of. Since the Scary Gun Police have deemed these rifles unfit for society and somehow determined that they are able to produce more death and destruction than a rifle without a pistol grip, I think we should call them ESRs (Extra Shooty Rifles). The wonderfully sarcastic Dana Loesch helped inspire that terminology. Read her stuff. She is a true Patriot.

Perry's "Wife Killer" comments help the world see that people like this don't take into account the effects their ridiculous ideas would have were they ever actually implemented into society. Take for instance the complete removal of Extra Shooty Rifles. It is a completely moot topic because it is physically impossible to ever remove these rifles, but if it were possible it would only change the behavior of those who obey the law. It would change hunting and firearm sports forever. It would put millions of businesses (large and small) out of business and crush small business owners and their families financially. It would put thousands of people in danger by eliminating their ability to protect themselves in their own homes and it would violate the rights of every single American citizen in order to make a political attempt at stopping a minute fraction of deaths in America. It wouldn't get to the cause of homicidal behavior and it would result in nothing more than a sickening violation on the good people of America.

I compare the regulation of guns to the concept of mandatory breathalyzers in all automobiles. In this scenario we would mandate that all cars sold in the USA be equipped with a breathalyzer ignition to prevent the operation of the motor vehicle by someone who is intoxicated. Remember, more deaths occur in cars than by guns. If the Anti-Gunners really wanted to prevent deaths, even if it could save *just one life*, they would put their focus on an area that would make a real difference. The reason they don't is because they understand the destructive effects a regulation like breathalyzer ignitions would have on the mass of people--themselves included. It would affect everything from commerce to the basic freedoms we enjoy in America. It would affect them on a personal level so they would never bring it up. The far reaching negative effects would be endless. Regulating guns however doesn't matter to them because it wouldn't affect them. At least they think it wouldn't affect them. Current gun restrictions already affect the Anti-2nd Amendment Radicals in a negative way but they just won't let themselves admit it, at least not in public. Ask yourself how many family survivors of "Gun Free Zone" killings supported GFZs prior to losing their loved ones in one of those death traps they helped create.

The hypocrisy and ignorance runs deep on this topic. As damaging as their false narrative and misleading rhetoric can be, it is entertaining and enlightening to watch the Anti-Gunners go to work in the media. Their tactics become obvious, yet their cheerleaders continue to cheer them on as they push forward with their agenda.

Much of the debates we hear in the media around guns and related topics are less about getting information to the public and more about the fiery rhetoric that inspires higher ratings. Yes, ratings. Let's not forget what's really going on here. Don't take your eye off the money ball. Do you really think they intend to resolve any issues in a three-minute piece with 4 guests? Pro-Gunners go on these shows with the hope and intent of spreading truth, logic and generally giving people real information they can work with. On the other hand, the Anti-2nd Radicals are focused on using every available second to infiltrate the conversation with key words and imagery that will bring the viewer to the dark side of the gun debate and create a false and negative narrative. I must admit, it's troubling to watch at times but when you recognize it at least you know what's going on.

When it comes to guns in the media, mainstream has pretty much given up on even pretending to want a balanced debate anymore. This is why you'll see networks like MSNBC not even offer a seat to a pro-gun advocate or worse, put in someone who is said to be pro-gun but is still on the other side. They'll forego an honest conversation just to fill the time with 100% anti-gun rhetoric served up by fast talkers with boisterous personalities. It serves their need, keeps their viewers cheering and keeps them safe from being schooled or held accountable for the false narrative they have been pushing over the years. Oh yeah, and it makes their advertisers happy. On the other hand you may catch some honest debate from conservative news radio, cable outlets like FOX, and some networks who still believe in fact-based journalism.

When we talk about the narrative that is created around guns, we also understand that other areas of our culture are misrepresented as well. Ever since President Obama said the Cambridge police "acted stupidly," law-enforcement has been dragged through the mud. Have comments like this encouraged disrespect or violence toward our LEOs? Demonizing cops and demanding their indictments for simply doing their job and protecting society from dangerous criminals seems to be a national pastime. We have allowed a fringe element of an anti-law enforcement portion of our society to run away with a destructive and misleading narrative that paints police officers as the Bad Guys. With the empowerment of the media and anti-cop rhetoric from some Mayors, DAs and the President & his staff, the people who vow to defend us have been put on trial and have to now defend themselves.

My experiences with law-enforcement have always been good so as I watch the anger directed against them I wonder how people can propagate such negative imagery. I thought it would be appropriate to get the perspective of law-enforcement with respect to guns in society and the mindset of the men and women behind the badge so I asked Officer Stan Lenic to participate in an interview. The intent was to help people see what is really going on in the minds of police officers and to cut through all the rhetoric with a straight interview. Officer Lenic has been a police officer for 9 years, is a member of the Capitol District Forensic Haz-Mat team, and a certified fire investigator. He has always been an advocate for the rights of the people. He even made the news and created quite a stir when he defended the 1st Amendment right of privacy advocates against the overreach of authorities at the Albany International Airport in 2012. I found the interview with Officer Lenic to be encouraging and quite contrary to what you might hear from anti-cop groups. Especially the ones who blame police officers for unfair treatment while simultaneously burning down their own cities.

Over coffee at Panera Bread in Glenville, NY on January 8th, 2016 Officer Stan Lenic and I had the following conversation.

DW: Why did you get into law-enforcement?

SL: Well, a few reasons. I have always had compassion toward children and animals and I always got angry when I would see people abuse those who can't defend themselves. I want to be a voice for them, to protect them. You talk to a lot of police officers and they may say, "This is always something I've wanted to do." But when you really look at it, you realize that you really do like people and just want a well balanced, organized society. I also want to protect the people who are productive members of society. Because let's face it, crime typically comes from those who are not productive members of society. I have the utmost respect for people who are productive, you go to work every day, you take care of your family, you earn a living and you don't put others at risk. In this country you can do those things and have the nice house, nice car and a great life. That's the American Dream. But some people get side-tracked and think there's a faster way to get there and that's when they get involved in crime.

Good Gun Bad Guy

DW: What's your biggest fear when you go out on a call?

SL: I never really thought about it. In this line of work, you're always running toward the chaos when everything in your body tells you to go in the other direction. It's the fight or flight instinct. You know that internal, Neanderthal emotion. We, as police officers, fire fighters, EMS, we go toward the danger. You saw it on 911, you saw it in Boston, you saw it in San Bernardino.

DW: So what is it that causes you to do that? Is it your training? Is it something you have internally before you even enter the police force?

SL: I guess if you look at it, it's something that can't be taught. People in emergency services are typically type "A" personalities. They are likely to take charge. If an incident happens, they're the ones who say, "We need to do this and this..."

DW: Sounds like they're leaders.

SL: Yes. They are leaders. Absolutely. I don't think about the fear of it. I don't think, "If I go to work today, am I coming home?" Of course we are aware of the dangers, we're just not scared of them. We've had extensive training and know that it's our job to run toward the sound of gunfire. I don't really think about it. It's not something that really goes through my mind.

DW: Do you see any dangers with military style rifle bans or restrictions for civilians?

SL: The 2nd Amendment says your right to bear arms shall not be infringed. It's a short clause.

DW: It also talks about militia.

SL: Yes it does. Things tend to be cyclical. If we look back to the American Revolution we see that at that time we were trying to break away from England. That's why we have the Constitution. It's because we wanted to be free of tyranny. In my opinion we are starting to get back to that again. It seems we are getting to that with our current Commander in Chief (Barack Obama). You won't solve the problem of violence by taking the guns away. Disarming people only creates more victims. Bad Guys are going to commit their crimes and violent behavior where people are the weakest. As for military style weapons, you get the argument from the left that says, "Back then, all they had were muskets." Well, that was the most advanced technology at the time. I'm sure the smartest guys back then had the forethought that technology would change. I'm sure when they wrote the Constitution they realized the technology would change.

DW: So, in current times it would seem that the Anti-2ⁿᵈ Radicals would prefer we be limited to the technology we had back then. I wonder if they would be willing to go to work in a horse-drawn buggy.

SL: Exactly.

DW: So it sounds like you're saying our rights should apply to current technologies.

SL: Yes. They must keep up with technology. I also believe there should be some organization. In other words, if you're gonna' carry, you should have a pistol permit and you should be trained. I know the 2ⁿᵈ Amendment is our pistol permit, but good training is essential. Getting guns out of the hands of the mentally ill is our priority. Let's face it, they're committing the violent gun crimes. Owning a pistol or rifle is a huge responsibility and someone who carries a pistol with them all the time should have proper training. I went through extensive training on how to handle a firearm, the safe use of a firearm and the proper way to fire a firearm, whether it be a pistol, a rifle, or a shotgun. More than the typical training required to get a pistol permit.

DW: Is it fair to say that you would not be opposed to a more extensive training for people who wanted to carry a gun?

SL: Absolutely. I think rather than implementing infringing laws, there should be more training and productive things done. Here's an example. For instance the SAFE Act in New York. Here's a law that was passed in the middle of the night, a very shady way of doing it and at the time they didn't even account for police officers. So any police officer carrying more than seven rounds could be arrested for criminal possession of a firearm, because they failed to put that clause in there. Of course a police officer is carrying more than seven rounds but it (the NY SAFE Act) didn't exclude police officers.

DW: The seven round thing for civilians died correct?

SL: Yes. It's now ten rounds.

DW: Funny how they didn't publicize the failure of that magazine capacity attempt.

SL: So the SAFE Act was not thought out. It was pushed through without any thought, any research and that's what I think the majority of the people are upset about; that it was pushed through in haste without any thought or consultation with law enforcement. There is a whole gamut of things that need to be looked at and studied before making a hasty, reactive decision that will affect everyone. I also think there should be a twilight on laws like this. In other words, at a certain point the law gets re-evaluated. If it's working, reinstitute the law. If it's not working revise it. If someone is walking around with no permit, carrying a 40 caliber, loaded with fifteen rounds and one in the chamber, that's someone who should get charged with the Safe Act. But Dan Wos, going to the range with his pistol locked in a case, magazines out, no rounds in the firearm, has his pistol permit, with a corresponding serial number and a couple boxes of ammo, I say, have a good time. If I pulled you over, I'd say Mr. Wos, have a nice day.

DW: Since you brought it up, let's talk about a typical traffic stop with a licensed concealed-carry driver.

SL: From a law enforcement perspective if I pulled you over, I'd like to see hands on the wheel and know up front if you had a firearm in the car. "Officer, this is what I have, I'm going to reach into my back pocket to get my driver's license and pistol permit. The gun is in the glove box or backseat." Or wherever it is and it's locked. Or, if you are carrying, that's something we need to know about as a police officer.

DW: People are often concerned about what to do if they are pulled over while carrying.

SL: If you're legally carrying, you get pulled over and you have a concealed-carry permit, the first thing you should do is roll all your windows down, turn your interior lights on, turn your vehicle off and place your keys on the dash. You should have both hands on the top of the wheel because the one thing a police officer is worried about is your hands. The officer will do his normal greeting and ask for your license and proof of insurance. The first thing out of your mouth should be, "Officer, I have a pistol permit, it's in my back pocket, I am carrying my licensed pistol at this time and it is located on my right hip (or wherever it's located).

DW: Should you add specifics like "It's loaded, nothing in the chamber..." things like that?

SL: Definitely because the more information a police officer has, and you being honest and up front with him, it lowers his nervous factor. Then he will give you instruction on what to do next. He may want you to reach into you back pocket for your driver's license and pistol permit. After you do what he asks, put your hands back on the wheel. He's going to explain to you why he stopped you. "I stopped you for speeding, traffic light, whatever." I've had numerous contacts with civilians that were carrying and they were very respectful. In my experience anyone that was a pistol permit holder was honest, polite, respectful and basically did everything I asked them to do.

DW: Are there any situations like that when the officer would want to take possession of the gun or do they typically give you the ticket and send you on your way?

SL: We would like to verify the serial numbers, so we would probably ask you to exit the vehicle, place your hands on the vehicle and we would secure the weapon, remove the magazine and make sure it's cleared. Once we're done with our interaction with you, we'd hand you back your weapon with the slide locked back and the magazine removed.

DW: So you're saying that's pretty typical?

SL: Yes and that's not to imply anything bad about you, it's just for our own safety. To be clear, we're not taking possession of your weapon, we're just checking and verifying for our safety and your safety. Any responsible gun owner would not have a problem with that.

DW: What are some of the things you do to evaluate whether or not a person may be a threat?

SL: Furtive movements, someone who's trying to conceal something quickly, nervousness, shaking, sweating and repeating my questions.

DW: Really? What do you mean?

SL: When someone repeats my question back to me they are often stalling for time to think of a lie. Like, "Do you have a weapon on you?" "Do I have a weapon on me?"

DW: OK. I see. It gives them a little time.

SL: Yes. Of course law enforcement officers that have been doing this for a long time know what questions to ask. They know what questions will pique interest and they know what answers are those of people trying to hide something.

DW: With all the racial accusations and attempts at controlling people with Political Correctness, are you able to identify someone based on race, color and gender?

SL: Yes. We will stop someone based on whatever information we are given by the person calling it in.

DW: I would hope you'd be able to.

SL: Yes, because you are describing somebody. It may just be a man wearing a white shirt and jeans, but the description may very well include race gender and anything else.

DW: With respect to traffic stops, is that detainment? Because I have seen people who think they can leave and the officer has no right to hold them.

SL: When you are pulled over in a traffic stop, you are being detained because the officer has most likely seen a violation. You are not free to leave. The officer needs a reason to stop you and has seen something with his own eyes. If at any time during a traffic stop someone believes they are free to leave, they are dead wrong. Whether or not he has probable cause to search is another thing. At that point we are getting into the 4th Amendment.

DW: Let me shift gear a bit and ask you, how would it feel to go out on a call without your gun?

SL: I wouldn't want to do it. Police officers are equipped to be prepared for what weapons might be out there. They have weapons to protect themselves. The reason we carry what we do (and I won't get into specifics) is because of events that have happened in the past.

DW: So it sounds like being equipped with adequate firepower to combat the opposition is necessary. Not carrying is not even an option.

SL: That's right. Do you want to carry a pen knife to a sword fight? For me to go out into the streets without a shotgun, patrol rifle or duty weapon is not something I would want to do. Look at the bank robbers in California that were wearing body armor. Pistols weren't even penetrating. These guys were taking hits like crazy.

DW: So, let me ask you. Do you think the 2nd Amendment is necessary?

SL: This is the greatest country in the world. We are a gun nation and the idea that we have the 2nd Amendment is amazing. I would not want to live in England.

DW: I agree. That brings me to the next question. What are your thoughts on more people getting their concealed-carry licenses? Obviously they are increasing in numbers. Black Friday 2015 had the most handgun background checks in any one day ever in the history of America.

SL: I think as long as you go through the background check, go through the application process and that you are a responsible gun owner, your 2nd

Amendment right shall not be infringed.

DW: So you look at it as more of a 2ⁿᵈ Amendment right rather than people being able to defend themselves before calling you?

SL: That's an interesting question. Let me give you a scenario. You have an active shooter in a mall. We don't get a report that a good guy is on the scene and has a gun and is actively engaging the shooter. We're coming in and you have someone trying to do the right thing by engaging the active shooter. Now you're getting into a very tense situation between law enforcement and a concealed-carry permit holder. That information needs to be relayed to the police department with a description of the good guy with a gun.

SL: So are you saying that with respect to a good guy on the scene with a gun it could potentially muddy the waters?

SL: I'm saying that each scenario is different and mass situations are filled with chaos. It's our job to make order out of chaos and the more information we can have, the better off we are. We need as much information as we can get going in to a situation.

DW: I can imagine the stress. Which would you prefer from your perspective, concealed or open carry for civilians?

SL: Its six in one, half dozen in the other. Let's look at Texas. They just passed their open-carry law.

DW: That just happened last week.

SL: Yes. Now you as a bad guy, walking into Panera bread like the one we're in now, and you see three guys with holstered weapons, you're probably not going to do anything. You might think twice. But then again, when I'm off duty, I would like the element of surprise. As a

87

civilian and given a scenario of witnessing a robbery in a convenience store, I would rather surprise the bad guy and give him an opposition he was not expecting. I'm 50/50 on this because we could sit here all day and talk about different scenarios where open would be better than concealed and vice versa.

DW: What is the best part of your job?

SL: Helping people. I went to a call once, single mom, her boyfriend was violent toward her and she had three kids in the house. I thought, these poor kids are walking around with full diapers, nothing in the fridge except a quarter gallon of sour milk. This was around Christmas time a few years ago. I went to the store. I got milk, eggs, bread, some cold cuts, peanut butter and jelly and brought it up to her. She was so thankful. She said, "Oh my God, thank you. You don't know how much this means to me."

DW: So that's the good stuff?

SL: That's the good stuff. Another example was when another officer and myself went on a call where a person had overdosed on heroin and we carry the medicine to bring them back. So we go on this overdose call and this kid was checkin' out. He was blue, lips and everything. We gave him the medicine to bring him up out of it and basically saved this guys life. We got there before the paramedics did.

DW: I heard that stuff is pretty amazing.

SL: It is. It's the things like that. People don't always expect cops to help.

DW: It sounds to me like you guys need to be somewhat hard and calloused when it comes to your job, but you also like the opportunity to do those caring deeds and help people when they really need it most.

SL: We're not just police officers. We're social workers, mentors, counselors, sometimes an EMT and sometimes a firefighter. We wear many hats. A lot of people think, "Oh a police officer, they arrest you and take you away." It's not like that.

DW: What about the repeat offenders, the guys who you arrest over and over for the same thing. Do you start to lose compassion for them?

SL: Yeah, for whatever reason, they keep doing what they do. You can only tell them so many times, "Look, you gotta try something new, something different, a new job." You get tired of helping them out because they don't make any changes. It's like, "How many breaks do I have to cut you before you wake up and get your head out of your ass?"

DW: Well, thanks so much. I really appreciate your time and all the great insightful information.

SL: No problem at all. It was my pleasure.

Good Gun Bad Guy

3.RECRUITING THEIR MINIONS

"What luck for rulers that men do not think."

-Adolf Hitler

Bernie Madoff (the Ponzi King) convinced the people of future investment benefits to serve himself. All his misleading information and encouragement was based on false data. When he was finally caught, the remaining wealth that was left was redistributed and given back to the rightful owners but it was too late. There was very little left. The people who trusted him and gave him their life-savings lost. The warriors who supported him and believed every word he told them lost everything. They weren't paying attention to the game. They only believed the hype. The people who blindly follow leaders and assume they have the best interest of the people in mind, become pawns in the game. They are often manipulated and led to believe they are doing the right thing. Leverage is used to achieve the support of the warriors. Most often it is psychological leverage in the way of guilt, fear and anger.

We have liberal-progressive leaders and we have liberal-progressive followers. The liberal-progressive followers are the ones we Americans fight on a daily basis as we try to show them how they are being misled and sold a destructive bill of goods. The leaders sit back and watch as they feed their warriors.

91

The arguments between pro-gun Americans and Anti-2nd Amendment Radicals will probably go on forever but understanding some key distinctions will help real Americans handle the Radicals in a respectful and productive way. What's happening to Anti-Gunners is very complex and will take consistent reinforcement to undo the terrible injustice that has been perpetrated on them. Remember, beliefs are developed most often as a result of repetitive data entering the brain. When we are told something over and over it sinks in and eventually becomes part of our thought process. It's why you put your seatbelt on as soon as you get into the car or why you may wait twenty minutes before going into the pool after eating. Some beliefs may be valid and protect us while some beliefs may be debatable.

It's very difficult to change someone's opinion on a topic if they truly believe in their cause. In this case, the Anti-Gunners truly believe they are fighting the good fight. They have been sold a very dishonest bill of goods through the use of propaganda, rhetoric and fear-tactics. They are also reminded what a dangerous world it would be if they don't keep up the fight. As a matter of fact they see what a dangerous world it would be every time a mass-killing occurs. Once they feel the angst, they are programmed to believe that it is because of guns. They believe guns are the cause and they have a lot of hard work ahead of them if they ever want to defeat this horrible monster. They must be vigilant so they continue to push forward with their agenda. They are told they are doing the right thing and if they waiver or relent, their cheerleaders are there to remind them, immediately following the next massacre, how serious their fight is. They are told the choices they are making by pursuing the fight to end "gun violence" is making a difference and their hard work is paying off but they have more work ahead of them. Some people fall for it and some don't. The ones who fall for it will argue to the death to validate their position because being wrong cuts to the core of their character and exposes their gullibility.

If you want to recruit people and get them to fight for your cause, you must either give them something in exchange for their efforts or convince these potential followers in a compelling way that the cause is valid. You must convince them in a way so their drive and passion for the cause is unstoppable. The people at the helm of the gun-control agenda know this and will use any and all tactics that are available to them in their pursuit to recruit as many voters.. er, I mean people as possible. This is why Eric Holder said the following:

"I've also asked the school board to make a part of everyday some kind of anti-violence, anti-gun message; every day, every school, at every level. One thing that I think is clear with young people and with adults as well, is that we just have to be repetitive about this. It's not enough to simply have a catchy ad on a Monday and then only do it every Monday. We need to do this every day of the week and just really brainwash people into thinking about guns in a vastly different way." – Eric Holder, 1995

Yes, he really said that.

But Eric Holder is certainly not the only one. These persistent attempts to brainwash anyone who will listen have been going on for a long time. On February 3, 1989 an article called "Epidemiologists Aim at New Target: health risk of handgun proliferation" was written in the Journal of the American Medical Association. In the article Dr. Patrick O'Carroll, then an official with the CDC's Epidemiology Branch's Division of Injury Control spoke out against private gun ownership when he said,

"The way we're going to do this is to systematically build a case that owning firearms causes death."

Also In 1993, Katherine Kaufer Christoffel, chairwoman and founder of the Handgun Epidemic Lowering Plan (HELP) conference recognized the power of attacking people psychologically.

It would appear that her intent was to use their personal vulnerabilities, in this case "being accepted by their peers," as leverage against them. According to HELP, the conference's goal was to bring together, *"like-minded individuals who represent organizations interested in using a public health model to work toward changing society's attitude toward guns so that it becomes socially unacceptable for private citizens to have handguns."*

These are just a few of the many admissions of intent, by Anti-2nd Amendment Radicals, to convince people to believe what they want them to believe. It's important to note that these people understand that belief-altering tactics must be used to ultimately achieve their political goals. It would also appear, that to them, mind-manipulating strategies are fair game. Apparently it's not ok to have beliefs that contradict the Anti-Gun Radicals and if you do, there will be tactics used to convert you to their way of thinking.

The pro-gun mentality has been a big part of our culture since we first became a nation. Guns are literally why we are here. If it wasn't for guns we would not be the United States of America. Without guns to overtake the British there would be no America. The Anti-2nd Radicals don't allow this to become part of the conversation or part of their thought process because it goes against what they have been taught to believe. If it does come up, they quickly dismiss it by using the rebuttal that we are now living in different times. Whatever that means. Sure, technology has changed the way we live but human nature is quite the same as it has always been. The reason they think the way they do is because they have been leveraged by liberal ideology and the Democratic wing of our government.

The belief that gun ownership must be highly restricted by government and eventually banned is developed in the minds of some by capitalizing on three very important human traits; fear, the need to win and the inherent need to pick sides. We all know that when we are scared, we will do whatever is necessary to protect ourselves from danger. What many people don't realize about fear, is that it is created by a lack of information or data. Acquiring the necessary data always relieves the sense of fear.

The anti-gun movement continually perpetuates and reinforces fear in the minds of its people by using the media. Every day you can bet you'll see some form of scary gun activity in the news. Typically following the scary gun activity will be some talk about gun laws and what we need to do to put more restrictions on gun owners so this never happens again. You'll usually see a Pro-Gunner and Anti-Gunner debating over what should be done and the effectiveness of current gun laws on the news but they don't focus on the cause of the problem. They only focus on the gun because banning guns seems a heck of a lot easier than addressing the minds of maniacs or those that are mentally disturbed. Plus, it makes for better TV. Mental instability is never addressed. If it is mentioned in relation to some violent act, it gets over-looked and the topic quickly moves back to the gun.

Mentally incompetent people can pass gun purchase background checks because politicians have not yet demanded they be put into the National Instant Check System (NICS). This is why we have killers passing background checks. The politicians who are supposed to be looking out for our best interest won't tell you that. They would much rather add more restrictions to gun ownership and further burden the law-abiding citizens. By enforcing the laws and using the resources we already have, we could make a big difference in gun-related crime. In other words we could actually prevent the Bad Guys from getting guns.

How could a mental disorder *not* be the cause of someone purposely killing innocent people?

Good Gun Bad Guy

Yet they still find a way to justify blaming the gun. The people watching these anti-gun media blasts go through the typical cycle of fear & anger and then are given the solution, all within a 3 minute news piece. It's brilliant and actually very easy once you understand how to stimulate and guide the thought process of passive-thinking viewers to a desired belief.

Next is the need to win. We all want to win. It's inherent in almost everything we do from climbing the corporate ladder, to picking a Super Bowl team, to being the first off the line at a red light (maybe that last one's just me). The media and anti-gun propagandists put people against each other using our inherent need to win as leverage. They do this by creating competition. The liberal media will show footage of pro-gun Americans exercising their right to open-carry just to infuriate the anti-gun crowd and the conservative media will make sure you see the Anti-2nd Radicals picketing in front of a gun shop in Riverdale, Illinois. This is done to build animosity. It's done on both sides of the argument because if you want to win, you must first pick a team.

Although Anti-Gunners never want to talk about the real problems like; maniacs, human anger or incessant radical Islamic violence, they sure do like to play "gotcha." They would much rather give you a good "zinger" and leave you scrambling for a rebuttal to some ridiculous piece of ant-gun data then talk about the real issues and causes of senseless violence. The truth is, they don't know where to begin when it comes to human violence. Besides, guns scare them so badly that they just want to see them go away. Condemning guns helps them feel a bit of strength in an area where they normally feel helpless and weak. The Anti-Gun Minions just want anything that scares them or gives them opposition to just go away. Their answer is to ban it! The Cheerleaders however, want control.

Do you think people are more likely to support a ban on

something because it is dangerous or because it is socially unacceptable? Think about it for a minute.

How hard have you seen people work at banning cars or cigarettes?

In 2010, 32,999 people died in car crashes in the United States alone. I don't remember seeing a "Moms Against Cars" group. I do know that there are some circles that would like to see gasoline powered cars go away. I'm just not sure that it's in support of saving lives as much as it is in support of a liberal agenda.

How much effort have you seen put into banning cigarettes?

This one is a little different because as cigarettes become less socially acceptable they are starting to go underground. Smoking is no longer allowed in public places in some states and there is a general feeling of disdain toward smoking. Is that because they kill people or because non-smokers are becoming less tolerant? In the 60's and 70's cigarettes were cool, or should I say "Kool." Now, not so much. Cigarettes are increasingly becoming socially unacceptable so you are starting to see them slowly disappear. Does it have anything to do with the fact that they cause on average more than 480,000 deaths per year in America, or is it because they are not so socially accepted anymore, or is it something else? Regardless of the reason, you don't see negative propaganda denouncing cigarettes and cigarette smokers like you do with guns.

Many people would like to see cigarettes go away but you just don't see a big public push for it. I haven't seen a "Moms Against Cigarettes" group yet. Maybe the reason cars and cigarettes are not banned (even though they cause a combined total of over a half million deaths per year in America) is because they generate huge money via taxes on both State and Federal levels. Think about how much state sales tax is collected on a $25,000 collector car if it

97

exchanges hands 10 times over the course of its life. The answer is $20,000 if the interest rate is 8%.

A perfect example of how people rally behind a cause that reflects upon them socially (rather than something that puts them in real danger) would be the push for "Political Correctness." In the case of political correctness we have seen groups form and rally, we have seen people lose their jobs for saying something that went against the new acceptable terminology and we have even seen "Safe Zones" created for whiny college kids who can't handle opposing opinions. Yet, I haven't seen or heard of one single death caused by any word in the English language. And, you ready for this?....free speech is protected by the Constitution!

The Anti-2nd Radicals have done, and continue to do, everything possible to make guns socially unacceptable because they know people are more likely to refute something that reflects on their moral character rather than the safety of people. The moral character of people can often be shaped in part by the environment they live in and the narrative around them. Many people just don't want to be the minority so they bend to public opinion to avoid being on the wrong side of the issue.

Q: "What about banning something because it is dangerous?"

A: "That's an important thing to look at but not quite as important as what people will think of me as a person if I'm on the wrong side of a social topic."

The truth is, car related deaths and cigarette related deaths each far outweigh gun related deaths. Yet, the push to make guns socially unacceptable is fierce.

FBI-Number of gun related deaths in America (2012): 8,855
IIHS-Number of auto related deaths in America (2012): 33,561

CDC-Average number of cigarette related deaths per year in America: 480,000

The minions will follow the narrative they are given, despite the facts. Why? Because they don't have the strength to go against the ridicule and punishment they would receive from their own side. They know how fierce *they, themselves* can be and they would never want that fury turned on them.

The recruitment strategies of liberal-progressivism became perfectly clear to me one day when I was shooting with a good friend of mine. I was at the gun range with my friend Blake. We were talking about world news, what's going on with our country, the economy and how Democrats are nibbling away at the edges of our gun rights by implementing countless laws, restrictions and regulations. You know, the things concerned Americans talk about.

Blake's son Trevor was with us. Trevor is a young millennial of let's say the "Hipster" persuasion or what some proudly identify themselves as "Beta Males." Trevor is a bit socially awkward. He's wearing sandals at the range, kinda' feminine, has no interest in shooting and generally doesn't fit in but Blake wants nothing more than to do father-son things with his boy. So in the hopes of connecting with his son, Blake attempts to create these bonding moments.

The problem is Trevor has a very difficult time building rapport with people and always has his face in his phone. As the conversation evolved into the topic of our Constitution, Trevor chimed in and started to tell us how right-wing religious tyrants created the Constitution. I was shocked to hear him speak at all, but even more surprised by *what* he was saying. Blake asked him where he heard such a thing and Trevor told Blake that is was common knowledge and that his Dad should really bone up on a little history once in awhile. Talk about losing connection with your own son.

Trevor didn't know a thing about the Constitution but had a lot of opinions and this started to make Blake a bit concerned. I could see fear and embarrassment in my friend's eyes as he attempted to talk some sense into his son. The mood quickly went down-hill and we wrapped things up and went home.

For the rest of the day, I couldn't help but think about what happened at the range and I wondered how it is that our young people have fallen so easily for the left-wing progressive propaganda. My thought is that it is easier for them to latch on to that group and ideology because it promises many things that they would otherwise have to work for. Things like an entitlement mind-set, which is needed to convince oneself that it's ok to live with your parents and not work for a living and a feeling of being smarter and superior to others. Being liberal also allows people the comfort of feeling like a victim and the luxury of complaining about being offended while demanding everyone else accommodate them on social issues and pander to their whining.

There is also a false sense of safety that is built in to the movement. Some Universities are even creating "Safe Zones" where students can go if someone says something that they may consider offensive. These zones are created under the guise of safety with an implication that those who disagree with the liberal-progressive ideas may become violent. The liberal movement has a particular focus on the feelings of students these days. It is being taught that if someone says something that they disagree with, they do not have to stand for it. They can either go to their "Safe Zone" or protest against the person to shut them down. It's important to note that the "feelings" that are important are only those of the liberal-minded student and countering opinions are being labeled as "aggressions." The term "micro-aggression" is an extension of an "aggression" but is used when it is impossible to justify any aggressive disagreement at all. The term is used when a hint of contradiction may or may not be present. This is a beautifully crafted strategy by which anger, self-righteousness, leverage and labeling is used to manipulate free thinking and speaking people to get them to conform. It also paints the non-liberal as a dangerous person. The accuser's actions are justified by creating the appearance that protecting the feelings and safety of people is the accuser's intent. It is really just a way to stifle the free speech of anyone who disagrees with the accuser and it is designed to take away a person's right to free speech if the views being expressed are not what the liberal-progressive finds acceptable. Liberalism has it all, you would think.

Liberalism has gone so far off the deep end that within the progressive culture it is expected behavior to blame all of America's ills on the traditional white American male. But wait. In place of the strong, confident, dominant male there is a new "Beta-Male." These are men who refuse to embrace the concept of the traditional male persona. Instead, they take an approach and attitude toward the world that is intended to not offend, emasculate or dominate anyone in anyway. It is another form of ignorance. It attempts to ignore the responsibility to stand up and protect oneself or others. The beta-male (opposite of alpha-male) makes gender equality a priority and strives to blend in as a non-confrontational entity. The idea behind this movement is that men have been far too dominating and now is the time for a passive equal temperament among the sexes.

Although Liberals believe this is an empowering new way of life, what the liberal movement really does is rob some people of their own self-respect. It takes away their power to recognize their own self-worth, their ability to be proud of a job well done and the empowering feeling of standing up for true American values - values that made this country great. So while these young gender-neutral intellectuals are pouring lattes, working to perfect their feminine demeanor and demanding that people stop recognizing gender, there are other young men out there who aspire to be men; strong, confident, proud men. Those are the guys who will grow up to understand accomplishment and pride. They are the ones who will take over management of this great country. They are the ones who will run the major corporations and actually do the hard work that will need to be done to succeed.

There are certain necessary things that must be done to achieve what we have come to know as the American Dream. Typically hard work with a sense of focused attention and persistence are the catalysts. It is shameful that some in our government and media can convince our young people that financial equality is something that they are entitled to without putting in equal effort or creating equal value. With the offerings of free college at the expense of tax payers and unjustified minimum wage increases at the expense of businesses (with no regard to profit & loss), we are watching total corruption, lies and misleading ideas permeate the minds of our youth.

I am scared for these liberal youngsters because I think they are being badly misled by a movement that does not have their best interest in mind and will ultimately leave them facing a cruel world without the tools necessary to make it. It's time we get back to recognizing the fact that men are men and women are women. It does nobody any good to blur the two. While these progressive kiddos are rallying against big business, gender inequality, unacceptable burger-flipping pay and guns, productive young adults are running away with the prize. It's kind of sad that the progressives think they are doing the right thing based on what their ideology dictates but the rest of us just view them as strange little characters

102

that seem to be missing the point.

As Americans it is our responsibility to guide this lost group. We need them to be productive. We need them to be proud. We need them to be strong, yet we have an ideological movement that is steering them in a different direction.

As misled as American youngsters can be with respect to ideology, so too can they be misled to believe that guns are bad and should be demonized. Social media is the perfect tool for Anti-2nd Radicals to preach their gospel and recruit their minions. They will stop at nothing to make their point. Sometimes it's hard to understand what their point is because their kicking and screaming just seems to be a bunch of angry rhetoric but their actions can truly be dangerous when followers radicalize under them. A radical anti-gun group called The Coalition to Stop Gun Violence really takes it to the next level by using a dangerous and malicious tactic called SWATing against gun owners and encouraging their misguided followers to participate.

SWATing is a tactic designed to bring SWAT teams and law enforcement officers to a fake scene for the sole purpose of abusing law enforcement, punishing unsuspecting victims and for some demented fun. The Coalition to Stop Gun Violence's misguided minions are now being encouraged to call 911 upon seeing anyone with a gun. The intent is to create a scene where cops show up and bring hyped fear and anxiety to an otherwise uneventful situation. This is done under the guise of "suspicious activity." The Coalition to Stop Gun Violence group asks their followers to make the call to 911 in order to create as much publicity out of nothing in the hopes of shedding bad light on legal law-abiding gun owners. The group has repeatedly reassured their followers that law enforcement will indeed show up, and to "just make the call." Yes, even in areas where open-carry is legal, the anti-gun minions are encouraged to call 911, report a suspicious person with a gun and justify it by "playing dumb." In other words they get away with it by claiming ignorance to the gun laws in that particular area. Nice, huh? This is the mentality we are dealing with; irresponsible people creating fear among citizens while simultaneously putting people in danger. Why? Their intent is simple; to demonize gun owners and instill gun related fear in the public.

Erich Pratt from Gun Owners of America said, *"anti-gun advocates are clearly frustrated. They want guns banned but they have been thwarted in the past, so they are looking for alternative means. They are inciting their radical base to turn their own neighbors in."*

The thing these Radical trouble-makers don't realize yet is that they are desensitizing police officers to the seriousness of actual calls. By sending law enforcement officers on wild goose chases to serve their twisted agenda, what they are really doing is occupying law enforcement resources and preventing officers from helping people who may truly be in danger. SWATing has also caused the death of one man who was shot by law enforcement after they arrived on a call. John Crawford of Beaver Creek Ohio was killed by police when he became the unsuspecting victim of a false SWATing call. According to Bearing Arms the false claim by a SWATer that Crawford was loading an assault rifle and pointing it at people ended up in him losing his life. Police Chief Louis Ross of Sentinel, Oklahoma was also shot while responding to a SWATing call. SWATing has been done in the past by many people for many different reasons but now that Anti-2nd Amendment Radicals are losing the battle in their hopeless war against guns, they have embraced this tactic and are using it against law-abiding American gun owners. Here are a few comments and responses from The Coalition to Stop Gun Violence's Facebook page to illustrate the misleading nature of this group.

CSGV: "We've sad it before and we'll say it again. If you see someone carrying a gun in public and have ANY doubts about their intentions, call 911 immediately. NEVER leave yourself, or your loved ones, at the mercy of loose gun laws that routinely arm individuals with a history of violence."

KD: "For those saying 911 operator ignores them, that didn't happen to me when I called them regarding someone with a gun in my local Kroger store. They responded within a few minutes. That said, if you see something, say something."

CSGV: "They will respond. Call."

JL: "They tried that in Colorado Springs. 911 operator dismissed the caller due to open carry law."

CSGV: They won't dismiss it next time, that's damn sure. Make the call."

MH: "But what if open carry is legal?"

CSGV: "They will respond to the call, legal or not, particularly in the wake of what happened in Colorado Springs. Make the call. Let law enforcement sort out the good guys from the bad guys."

This last response from The Coalition to Stop Gun Violence is particularly disturbing. It clearly shows malicious intent and a focused effort on misguiding their followers. In this post, MH is trying to be sure she is not doing something unlawful or misleading and "The Coalition to Stop Gun Violence" responds in a way that encourages the action anyway. Rather than do the right thing Anti-2nd Amendment Radicals choose the worst possible tactic, putting people in danger just to support their agenda. It's important that Pro-Gunners are aware of the devious tactics that are being used on a daily basis to mislead fearful people and put others in danger.

4. SIT AT THE POPULAR TABLE

For some, being accepted holds a much higher value than pursuing a moral standard.

Have you ever sat at the popular table? Me neither. But wouldn't it have been great, especially at a time when you were most vulnerable and lacked confidence? That's the reason we as kids want to sit at the popular table. *"Ah, I'm finally accepted. I'm one of them now."* The "Popular Table" is a synonym for being a part of a group or being accepted by others. Being accepted brings with it confidence, self-esteem and the feeling of security. Everyone wants those things. Remember that one kid who finally achieved the high honor of being allowed to sit at the popular table and instantly turned against anyone that was not popular? Even worse, maybe he turned on his one friend who had stood by him the entire school year. Maybe that friend was you.

Why did he do that? Was being popular (and all the other things that come along with it) more important than friendship and maintaining strong human ethics, morals and loyalty? The answer is yes. To him being accepted was a higher value in that moment. Being accepted can be the most important thing to some people. Some will sacrifice what you and I may consider high values to obtain the feelings that they have associated with acceptance. To some *feeling good* is the most important thing regardless of the unethical or immoral actions they may have to take to achieve it, and with

107

ignorance to the destructive affects those actions may have.

Remember that one or two kids that always sat alone, never had any friends and never seemed to fit in anywhere? Even worse maybe they were bullied. No one wanted to be that kid. It's lonely at the bottom and people know this. As adults we understand this phenomenon and we have compassion for the underdog. Well, some of us do. Some adults still have the need to be at the popular table and see no problem with disrespecting others in the process.

During their time of struggle, those kids at the lonely loser table were building something. They were building something strong--self-esteem. They were learning how to develop personal strength. I explore this topic in great depth in the *Empowerment* chapter of my book "Defining Success in America." Personal power comes from strong internal beliefs about our ability to move forward and create our own destiny. It also comes from having acquired the tools and resources to move forward in the world. The strongest of those tools and resources are within us. In life, we can only do the best we can with the tools that are accessible to us at the moment. The thing we need to remember is that some people can access those tools and some people can't. It's no surprise that kids will avoid the difficult path and gravitate toward what appears to be the easy road to confidence. What is really troubling and harmful to our society is when adults do it.

We can apply all the same feelings and emotions that the lonely middle school student endures to adults in our society. You know them, you interact with them every day and you may even recognize their behavior. If you've ever seen some of the reality shows that celebrate the lives of materialistic, crybaby adults who constantly blame each other for their own emotional instability, you'll know what I mean. I won't mention the names of the shows because they don't deserve any recognition for implying that this is acceptable

108

adult behavior. The point is that this emotional insecurity does carry over into adulthood and unfortunately some of these adults are influential in our society.

"If you agree with our views, you can join us at the popular table. If you don't, we will ridicule, punish and destroy you."

Because the media has influence over it's viewers it can create a "popular table." Anyone inclined to gravitate toward instant acceptance will adopt the beliefs of the people at the popular table. Remember, people inclined to need acceptance bad enough that they are willing to compromise their own personal ethics and safety may not have developed a strong internal set of tools. Many Anti-Gunners will trip over themselves to get a seat at the "popular table" when it comes to the topic of guns. They disregard logic in expectation of being part of this politically correct, media-backed society. By touting anti-gun beliefs, the media consistently injects these people with the unfounded righteousness they love so much. These are people that cheer at their TV when another piece of fabricated data is used to blame a gun for the act of a fellow human.

The people that orchestrate the charade are the ones you'll see on news channels promoting the latest politically correct trend. Whatever is en vogue that week, you can bet they'll be supporting it. If the trend is going in the direction of cop-bashing, they'll be in front of the cameras trying to make you feel compassion for the poor misguided criminals. They do whatever they can to justify the cop-killer's actions. They'll spin the narrative 180 degrees so you'll believe that the cops are the bad guys and the criminals have been the victims because society has been so cruel to them. These are people who have sold their souls a long time ago in exchange for face-time and a chance to sit at the popular table. To be clear, there are still some ethical news outlets and journalists out there but it seems they are becoming fewer and far between.

If in recent times you've felt like the lonely kid at the loser table fighting against the world and knowing that your ethics and morals are in the right place, you're not alone. You may feel like the outcast because everywhere you turn, the narrative is the opposite of what you know to be true. The war on guns has been designed to achieve exactly that. The war on guns has been created to make you look stupid for even thinking that guns could be a useful tool in society. It's been set up in a way so all the people who support the 2nd Amendment and gun ownership think they are all alone at the loser table. Perception is everything in this fight and because the media creates the perception, it's important to counter their actions at every turn regardless of how daunting a task it may seem.

So while the Anti-Gunners are flocking to the popular table where they are allowed to say anything they want regardless of whether their claims are true or not, the Pro-Gunners are scratching their heads wondering how they are getting away with the lies and when it became politically acceptable to denigrate our own safety while taking pride in putting our families at risk. As we stand there confused and angry, we begin to realize that what happens at the popular table is wrong. What we need to recognize is why people need that popular table and understand that the ones who create the popular table have no ethical problems with manipulating the weak-minded. Once we understand those two components we can start to make a difference.

Lets expose the ones who are manipulated. They don't even know they have been manipulated and they will argue to the death if you tell them they have been. Why? Because no one wants to think they have been taken for a ride. Especially someone who may not have access to the internal tools that create real self-esteem. Admitting they were wrong would be a crushing event. Think about it. Who are the people who accept responsibility in your life? They are typically the leaders. They are the ones who are confident to

110

begin with. They know that they will become stronger through their failures.

The people who sit at the popular table are there because they don't have to face the reality of personal responsibility because the popular table provides a faux environment for them. In other words, you will be "cool" if you jump on the anti-gun bandwagon because it's the politically correct thing to do right now. So every time they see gun bashing in the media they can say *"Yup, that's my group. We're winning."* If you contradict them in any way they will have an arsenal of fabricated statistics that you probably don't have the resources on hand to debunk. It's easier to be anti-gun because emotions trump facts *and* you get accepted at the popular table.

Now let's look at the Manipulator. The manipulators are the ones who create the narrative. They know the weak-minded and fearful will follow and they know the strong will fight them. They are smart in their narration and they present topics in a way that makes it necessary to pick one side or the other. If the hosts at the popular table allowed a middle ground on topics there would be no need for the popular table. Division is a necessity. Think about it. Would it be a popular table if everyone could sit at it. No. It's like a club. *"If you agree with the beliefs we support, then you are welcomed here. If you don't, you'll have to leave."* They need some to leave because without opposition there is no popular table.

The anti-gun left understands how important imagery is, so making guns "uncool" and making it "cool" to be against guns is very important in their crusade to enroll young people. Many Millennials are happy to swim in their petri dish and be the experimental generation because they feel welcomed and have no fear of confrontation being on that side. They gravitate toward that side because they are constantly told that if they denounce guns and push the anti-gun narrative they will be doing their part to create a safe environment for everyone. Pro-gunners are never the aggressors in this debate so the weak tend to pick the side that they think will experience the least amount of resistance. That's all beginning to change, but in recent years Pro-Gunners have made it a point to play the passive role while the Anti-2nd Radicals always seem to be the ones poking the bear.

A typically colorful narrative that always gets support from Anti-Gunners is the idea that all gun owners are unsophisticated, back woods, rednecks with a confederate flag flying from the bed of their jacked up pick-'em-up-truck and wearing over-alls. The notion that gun owners are stupid helps the Anti-2nd Radicals recruit the people who think they are (or want to be) ever-so-sophisticated and intelligent. Because what is worse than being labeled as a big dumb redneck if you are someone who strives to be recognized as a sophisticate? Again, this plays right into the need to sit at the popular table and because some people need to believe they are smart, sophisticated and important the "dumb redneck" narrative is a perfect tool to manipulate the weak-minded and lure them to the side that promises intellectual virtue. They can gather together and express their compassion for the "crazy, stupid gun people" and talk about how uneducated they are. This helps the Anti-Gunners believe that they are in a position of authority and it strengthens their belief that they know what's best for everyone. For those who don't feel they are in a position of authority, they can still be thankful that they are not part of the underclass group of "non-sophisticates." It's a perfect form of leverage and utilizes the insecurity of people in a brilliant way. The ironic part is the ones who think they are on the winning team (or sitting at the popular table) are actually the ones being manipulated. They just don't know it.

Rallying famous people to speak out against guns is a primary mission for groups like "Everytown" and "Moms Demand." Hey, it works. People listen to famous actors and actresses because they hold them in high regard. We watch their movies and come to feel acquainted with them even if we have never met them in person. We welcome them into our homes and laugh with them. We have them at our dinner table and even fall asleep with them. Although they may not be there in the flesh, the associations and connections we make with them can be very personal and special. Often times we may put on a favorite movie or show when we are in a particularly heightened state of emotion. This is extremely personal stuff and the people we see on the screen often times becomes a personality we admire and respect. The thing we sometimes forget is that what we see on the screen is not a real personality. We are aligning with a fake persona, an actor or an imposter. Yet in our minds, they are not only real to us, we also tend to trust what they say as authentic and authoritative.

So when it comes time for Michael Bloomberg and his anti-gun groups to influence as many people as possible and change their internal representation of guns and gun owners; what better way than to rally the most influential people in the country? As I watched the "Demand a Plan to End Gun Violence PSA" it appeared that these actors really felt what they were promoting. You would swear they were passionate about the cause. Don't forget, they're actors. They didn't come out and say "we want to inflict more gun restrictions on law-abiding gun owners," rather they named a number of mass killing sites repeatedly and dramatically. They also encouraged the viewer that it's time to demand action. Action against what exactly? Well, conveniently at the end of the commercial the viewer is directed to a website. After a few link clicks and some exploration of the website I realized it was just more of the same "We can do it," "We can end gun violence" rhetoric. They used a technique where each word in the sentence "We-can-end-gun-violence" was used repetitively and powerfully. It would seem the intent was a cheap attempt at anchoring the words into the minds of the viewers.

Although the website touts over 3 million supporters it never gives any real solutions to how they plan on ending this so called "gun violence." The whole thing seemed weak to me be but I also recognize the intent to instill fear and sadness in the followers. These are two very strong emotions and the easiest way to manipulate people.

So in the end, all the "Demand a Plan" campaign appears to do is further indoctrinate and reinforce a negative representation of guns in the minds of people. Some may find it disgusting. I recognize it as disgusting yet clever branding. Unfortunately it is the most unethical and immoral way of influencing people. Not only are viewers misled with false rhetoric, the actors have been misled and encouraged to participate in this fear and sorrow campaign. The actors have either been misled or they are so driven by money that they are willing to compromise their own ethics. I bring this up because many of the actors involved, have been in movies that glorify violence and/or guns. Maybe that too is all part of the plan. Don't get me wrong; I'm the last guy to condemn people for making money. I happen to be a big fan of it myself, but I believe in staying true to personal standards. In other words, practice what you preach.

Some of the actors in the "Demand a Plan to End Gun Violence" propaganda video include: Gwyneth Paltrow, Reese Witherspoon, Ellen Degeneres, Jamie Foxx, Jason Bateman, Selena Gomez, Chris Rock, Courtney Cox, Brooke Sheilds, Beyonce and Conan O'brien. I have enjoyed much of the work these fine actors have produced, so it is somewhat disturbing to see them take part in such a misleading piece of anti-gun propaganda. I don't necessarily blame the actors because they are swimming in the anti-gun pool. I do however, blame them for not seeking the truth.

The intent behind the anti-gun PSA is to create awareness that will cause law-makers to push for more gun control legislation and average citizens to vote for those law-makers. What the actors don't seem to get is the fact that they are not focusing on the problem. They use their celebrity to influence people who love them because of the work they have done in movies and TV, but the narrative they create is misleading. We all know that stricter gun laws would not have done a thing to deter the killings they speak of in the PSA. To the contrary it is irresponsible gun laws that contributed to the deaths of the innocent people involved. You guessed it; the infamous Gun Free Zone.

Among the mass-killings mentioned in the PSA were Sandy Hook, Newtown, Virginia Tech, Tuscon, Aroura and Fort Hood. Claiming that something needs to be done to stop mass killings like the one in Fort Hood is especially disturbing because Fort Hood is a military base. Where else would you have the most potential for defensive firepower and trained residents? You would think Fort Hood but in reality Fort Hood was deemed a Gun Free Zone and therefore converted into the most vulnerable situation possible. Under Democrat President Bill Clinton military bases became Gun Free in 1993. It should be noted that despite two mass killings Fort Hood remains a Gun Free Zone. If it infuriates you that celebrities and politicians can double-down on repeatedly failed policies like this, you're not alone. Logical thinking people scratch their head wondering how accomplished, successful, intelligent people can promote such ridiculous things, but it would seem that in our society celebrity trumps logic in many cases.

So why is it that gun owners seem to always be defending their rights and character to an ideology that relentlessly continues to create divisive positioning among people? The anti-gun argument comes off with a seemingly innocent justification. *"Why wouldn't gun owners support the ban of high capacity magazines, Gun Free Zones and background checks? We're only trying to make people safe,"* the Anti's say, hoping you'll see them as the ones with moral integrity. The argument is divisive in nature because while preaching the gospel of morality and rallying minions to their popular table, they are simultaneously setting the table to control and conquer the rights of the people.

When Eric Holder talked about brainwashing the people in 1995 he was setting the table for ten to twenty years in the future. He talked about changing the way children think because he knew they would be next in line to support the anti-gun agenda and keep Democrat politicians in office. It is now twenty one years later and those children are sitting at the popular table shaming gun owners and lumping them in with criminals as they talk about gun related crime in America. The idea that there is no differentiation between violent killers on the street and productive law-abiding gun owners when the topic of gun laws comes up is part of the strategy to increase the desire to sit at the popular table (or join the ranks of the Anti-2nd Amendment Radicals). The only people separating the law-abiding gun owners from the violent criminals within the conversation are the law-abiding gun owners. It doesn't serve the popular table to make that distinction because the more gun owners' reputations are tarnished, the more people will rush to sit at the popular table and shame their fellow Americans.

The subtle strategy of not differentiating the Good Guys from the Bad Guys is similar to the strategy of putting the focus on the gun rather than the human behavioral issues we have in the world. I talk more about this later but the idea here is to keep the focus on what they want the minions to see and keep what they don't want seen in the dark shadows. In other words,

"Look over here at all this gun violence, death and destruction. Oh, never mind the guy who wants to protect himself and his family. It's all the same thing. We just need to get rid of those damn guns."

Remember the saying, "Keep your eye on the ball?" There are a lot of deviant strategic moves being made at the popular table and the way they get implemented is by honest people assuming others will act ethically. The truth is, when it comes to this and other topics the ones who need to win will do and say whatever is necessary to change public opinion, shame gun owners and rally followers to their cause.

Good Gun Bad Guy

5. IGNORANCE IS BLISS

If a child covers his eyes so he can't see you, do you not exist?

Libby Left: Sir, I'm a little uncomfortable knowing that you have a gun on you.

Dee Fender: Well that must suck.

Libby Left: This isn't a joke Sir.

Dee Fender: I can tell. You're not laughing. Would it be better if you didn't know?

Libby Left: That's beside the point. The point is, you are carrying a gun and it makes me uncomfortable.

Dee Fender: Is it the gun that makes you uncomfortable or is it me?

Libby Left: I don't even know you.

Dee Fender: So it's the gun?

Libby Left: No, it's the idea that you could be some sort of maniac and shoot me.

Dee Fender: So, it is me you're scared of? Would you be scared of me if I didn't have a gun?

Good Gun Bad Guy

Libby Left: All I know is I shouldn't have to be forced into a dangerous situation just because you gun-nuts think this is the wild west.

Dee Fender: Let me ask you something. If the FBI were to run a background check on me, and it was determined that I have never in my life been involved in a serious crime or had any mental illness would that help you feel more comfortable with me?

Libby Left: There is no reason for people in this day and age to be walking around in public with guns.

Dee Fender: What if it were true that you are safer because I'm here; and what if it were true that in fact there are very good reasons for people to carry guns these days?

Libby Left: Oh, I suppose now you're gonna tell me how the world is full of terrorists.

Dee Fender: As a matter of fact there have been twenty-two terrorist attacks in the United States in the past two years. Two of them occurred in this State, along with nine thousand one hundred and sixty one violent crimes in this city alone. Those are only the ones that were reported. Ma'am your fear and anger is misguided. I suggest you open your eyes and start protecting yourself.

Libby Left: No thank you! I will not give in to the gun lobby and put myself at risk just so you right-wing crazies can run around town with deadly weapons just to get your kicks!

Dee Fender: Have a nice day Ma'am.

There are many ways in which ignorance is used to fabricate a case against guns. In fact ignorance *must* be used for people to continue their rhetoric amidst the countless accounts of guns being used by people to save lives. How is it that a seemingly productive, well-thought out person can ignore reality? If we look at the definition of ignorance, we find that it means to have a lack of knowledge. So, how is it possible for someone to *choose* to ignore data? It's not as much ignorance as it is lying to oneself. This is a complex topic but on the face of it we can see that "chosen ignorance" can be a very useful strategy when trying to prop up a corrupt agenda.

There have been many cases where people have encountered traumatic events and completely deleted any recount of the event itself. You may have heard stories of people who survived car crashes that took the lives of loved ones. The police and investigators are able to put together a nearly exact timeline and course of events while the person who experienced the crash first-hand doesn't remember a thing. It would seem that with a strong enough need, we as humans are able to delete data to protect ourselves. Maybe this is done to prevent any reoccurring horrors or maybe it's done to preserve our own integrity as we move forward in pursuit of a mission that we know is unethical.

When dealing with a person who chooses to ignore data it is a natural response to push the data at them. In other words, pile on actual data to counter their willful ignorance or stubbornness. We instinctively think that they don't know and it is our job to present them with the facts. Somehow they will then magically see the light and realize how uninformed they have been. Then all of a sudden they will come over to our side and begin supporting gun ownership and everyone will live in harmony once again. How often does this work? So why do both sides continue to throw data at each other? Let's first admit the fact that there is an instinctive need to win the battle. The Anti-2nd Amendment Radicals will never admit that, but we must at least recognize that there is an element of competition with respect to the topic of guns. Once we acknowledge that, we can start to see from their perspective. Once we see that along with fear and the need to be "right" they also have the need to "win." We all do. It's human nature. To Anti-2nd Radicals the topic of guns has turned into more a battle to win on a political level than it is about preserving life. If it were really about saving lives, they would denounce Gun Free Zones simply based on the number of killings that take place in them. That would be too logical and an admittance that they have been supporting a failed policy.

We must recognize the reality that facts really don't matter to them in this fight. Facts are just used as a tool to win the battle. When the real facts don't support their agenda, new facts can be created. All they have to do is eliminate a cross-section of society, narrow the geographic area of a study or simply state statistics based on hand-picked focus groups. Knowing that their main objective is to win helps us in countering the rhetoric and anger. You may ask yourself, what causes someone to need to win? That's the important part. That's the area that if focused on will bring real results. Everyone knows what it is like to win. Maybe it was a football game. Maybe you won a marathon. The feelings that come along with winning are tremendous. Conversely, the feelings that come with losing can be a real drag. This is why the liberal-left is trying to implement "participation trophies" into society. To some with less confidence, losing can be devastating. When you have a lot at stake and your credibility is on the line, you will do whatever it takes to avoid losing—sometimes even more than you will do to win. To some people the loss of credibility would feel like the end of the world. I remember watching an anti-gunner on TV (in reference to the NRA) screaming into a reporter's microphone at a rally, "We can't let them win!" As I noticed the fear, panic and anger in her eyes, I realized that to her this cause was about something other than saving lives. It was about winning.

This doesn't mean that we need to make this a competition. As a matter of fact, that would be counter-productive. But knowing a little bit about what is going on in the minds of Anti-Gunners will help us as we proactively push forward in our pursuit to defend decency, self-preservation and constitutional freedom for future generations.

Willful ignorance runs deep in the anti-gun world. I learned this first hand while trying to help a friend learn more about guns. My friend Derik started a gun conversation with me and seemed to have a genuine interest in learning more about them. This wouldn't normally be surprising but Derik is a very outspoken liberal and is the last person that I would have thought would bring up the topic of guns unless he was trying give me some anti-gun statistics. My first thought was, *"Alright what's the catch? Watch out Dan, you're walking right into it here."* But I engaged as if he were being authentic.

Keep in mind that Derik and I are friends but disagree politically on almost everything. He drives a Prius because he feels guilty about destroying the environment and I drive a Corvette because I don't buy the "man-made global warming" argument for a minute. He believes we should support the underclass by raising taxes on the people who produce and I believe we should give tax breaks to businesses so they can create more jobs. He believes in more rules and regulations when people do bad things and I believe in strengthening the moral ethic of people so they do the right thing. Our debates can be endless and very tiring. But we each understand that the other has the best intentions. Our opposition seems to come from structurally different thought processes, but each of our end-games are to arrive at solutions that will improve the lives of all people. What each of us thinks is better for people is like the difference between hot and cold.

Derik asked when I was going to take him to the gun-range. As you can imagine, my response was, *"Yeah right. You?"* But he was serious and convinced me that he really wanted to experience shooting first-hand. We talked about it a couple more times and I thought it might be an opportunity to show someone who wouldn't typically be inclined to shoot, how fun it really is. In the process maybe I could help him see the value in firearms for the purpose of protecting himself and his family. *"OK, I'll do it. I'll take Derik to the range."*

Before we went to the range and before I would consider putting a loaded pistol in his hands, I put him through an extensive safety training. He still talks about how responsible and articulate I am with respect to gun safety and training. I didn't do it because I wanted to show him how responsible gun owners are. I did it because I needed him to be calm and safe when we were at the range. I needed him to build a non-fearful respect for guns before we even considered live ammo. His acknowledgement of my respect for firearms was a happy coincidence. When I felt confident that Derik was clear on all safety measures I asked him to meet me at my house and I would take him to the range so he could finally shoot. On the day we went to the range he drove. He brought his Prius and there I was in the passenger seat. I still hear about it.

Aside from the ride in Derik's battery powered rollerskate, our experience at the range was a good one. Derik actually did very well and he even threw me a couple digs when he noticed me shooting off the mark. All in good fun and we went again within a couple weeks. He got the chance to interact with other shooters and seemed to fit in very well. Overall, I considered the whole experience a success. I was convinced that I had actually achieved what many pro-gunners want. That is, to help Anti-Gunners understand that the rhetoric and general narrative coming from the left is false and misleading. And that shooting and gun ownership is a good thing.

What happened later was very interesting and frustrating to me. I would eventually see Derik posting anti-gun propaganda on social media. Everything from bashing the NRA to the typical "guns kill people" rhetoric. He even made accusations that if it weren't for guns the Sandy Hook kids would be alive and he joked about the way gun owners live in daily fear for their lives as they cling to their guns. He posted memes depicting gun owners getting killed by their own guns and how ridiculous it is to think that carrying a gun is necessary. He was clearly fishing the networks for controversial responses and he would go on and on posting endless false gun data and statistics when people did take his bait. He was obviously on a frantic, angry, anti-gun mission. A very common thread within his posts was the strong need for government to regulate and control everything gun-related. In his posts, I sensed a spiteful tone and hatred toward people for having the freedom that the 2nd Amendment provides. I couldn't believe it was him posting this stuff. His attitude was so anti-gun that it made me cringe. Not just because I felt like I had been taken for a ride and tricked into devoting my time to thoughtfully training and educating him, but because I was beginning to realize that people (even those close to you) can be very deceiving. Especially those that want to see gun rights taken away. Is it possible he could have completely ignored his experiences at the range, all the great interactions with other shooters and everything he learned?

I believe Derik deceitfully conned me into bringing him to the range so he would have the knowledge and experience to be able to counter people if they accused him of never shooting a gun while preaching the anti-gun doctrine. I believe he was already so indoctrinated into the anti-gun camp that he put forth extensive effort and cost us both many hours so he could have an insider's view of the gun culture that he would later use to improve his game. I believe he did this so he could continue his mission with more tools. That's how strong a hold the Anti-Gun Radicals have over their minions. That is an example of how much positive knowledge people can have and still ignore reality. My point to the whole *Derik* story is that the mindset of the Anti-2nd Radical can be very rigid. In most cases they do not waiver. They can and do go to great lengths to support their position even if it means being dishonest. I don't mean to imply that Anti-Gunners are bad people but it is important to recognize that the Radicals fully believe and embrace the anti-gun narrative. Fear is the primary driver for some while the need to win drives others. Both are very strong human motivators.

Another dishonest tool that is frequently used to vilify guns is the creation of a false internal representation by using word associations. We often hear the old yet powerful term "gun violence" and we recognize that it is a clever way of creating word association to support a visual image in the minds of the unsuspecting viewers. Logically we know that the gun is not violent, but rather the person. The reason this term is used so often is because it is so juicy. When you hear the term "gun violence" what do you envision? You see a gun wreaking havoc on people. The fact that a *person* is being violent is the most powerful piece and it goes unnoticed. This is by design. Anti-Gunners know the term "gun violence" is misleading yet continue to use it anyway. That is a very productive tool in their toolbox. Picture the average non-gun owner sitting at the dinner table watching the news. How does he or she react when they hear the term "gun violence?" Well let's look at the word "violence." Inherently the word "violence" is something we want to avoid at all costs. What could be worse? Now attach anything you want to it and see what happens. How about "dog violence?" What do you envision? You probably see a dog attacking someone. If the media were to be honest, they would use the term "violence" or "violent behavior," but they like to attach the word "gun" to it.

In order to support their agenda of making guns bad while

simultaneously putting fear in the hearts of people they must set up the narrative in a way that vilifies the gun. The perpetrators of this narrative know that some people will be ignorant to the fact that violence is always caused by the person and not the gun. However, it is important to paint this picture in order to achieve their desired outcome. The imagery and emotion is the fuel behind their argument. Even if the data doesn't support the anti-gun claim, they hope to win you over with their emotional argument. A logical person would think that if you were to tout the notion that guns kill people, you would also have to support the fact that accidental deaths are caused by many other common activities as well, and most in much higher numbers.

- Overexertion - 10 per year
- Getting cut or punctured - 105 per year
- Bicycling – 242 per year
- Machinery – 590 per year
- Firearms – 606 per year
- Getting struck – 788 per year
- Other forms of transportation – 857 per year
- Pedestrian activity – 1074 per year
- Natural / Environmental – 1576 per year
- Fires / Burning 2845 per year
- Drowning – 3782 per year
- Unspecified – 5688 per year
- Suffocation – 6165 per year
- Falling – 26009 per year
- Poisoning – 33041 per year
- Automobile – 33561 per year

Fortunately for the progressive-radical-anti-gun crowd not everyone thinks logically and rationally. Often, decisions are made and beliefs are formed based purely on emotion.

Betty Bannit: Did you know that there are thousands of accidental gun deaths every year in America?

Carmen Sense: Actually the average is six hundred and six. If you were really interested in facts you would have known that.

Betty Bannit: And that is supposed to be a good thing? Even if it were only six hundred and six, I would think that is a good reason to ban guns.

Carmen Sense: Of course you would think that, because you don't take into consideration the fact that there are over thirty-three thousand accidental auto deaths in the U.S. every year and over twenty six thousand cases of people dying because of falls.

Betty Bannit: Excuse me, that's a little bit different.

Carmen Sense: You're right. It is different. It's different because restrictions on automobiles or climbing stairs would effect you in a negative way and would actually prevent unnecessary deaths, not cause more of them like gun restrictions. You wouldn't want that though.

Betty Bannit: Ok then, what about all the children getting guns and shooting people because irresponsible gun owners leave loaded guns just laying around the house all the time. This is an epidemic.

Carmen Sense: Hardly an epidemic but I understand your need for such colorful vocabulary. The truth is, and I'm sure you haven't heard this from your liberal media sources, that only eight percent of those accidental deaths are caused by children under six years old. That's a total of forty-eight per year. Not quite the amount of deaths you would like it to be or anywhere near the amount of deaths caused by drunk drivers, which is approximately ten thousand.

Betty Bannit: But why wouldn't you want to heavily restrict guns even if it could save just one life?

Carmen Sense: Because disarming good people by burdening them with more restrictions would leave them unarmed and helpless against attackers. That would cause even more death and violence because it would give the bad guys less of an opposition. Not sure what part of that you can't understand.

Betty Bannit: Oh, I understand all right. You think I don't care about people.

Carmen Sense: No, I think you avoid reality. If you allowed yourself to see the truth, you would put your efforts where they would be productive. Why are you not fighting to implement mandatory life-preservers for people within twenty feet of any body of water? Did you know that almost four thousand people in the U.S. drown every year? That's a heck of a lot more than the six hundred and six accidental gun deaths. You say you want to prevent senseless deaths but what you really want to prevent is the ability of people to own guns.

Betty Bannit: That's ridiculous.

Carmen Sense: What's ridiculous is your misguided understanding and lack of willingness to look at things in a logical way. By restricting guns you restrict all people's use of them. You don't care because you are not a gun owner. Mandatory life vests, safety harnesses for stair climbing or auto ignition breathalyzers would affect everyone in a negative way (including you), so you don't talk about that even though, if implemented, would save lives.

Good Gun Bad Guy

Betty Bannit: So... you want mandatory breathalyzers but everyone should be able to run around shooting each other with guns?

Carmen Sense: Not even close. Thanks though for showing me that you haven't heard a thing I've said and by the way, your violent anti-gun imagery won't work on me. Sometimes I wonder why we even allow you people into the conversation.

Betty Bannit: I am looking out for the safety of everyone.

Carmen Sense: Then why don't you lobby to put a law in place that would make it mandatory to wear a safety harness before climbing the stairs? Wouldn't it make sense even if it saved just one life?

To assume that the gun killed someone is ridiculous. You know that and I know that but the visual image in the minds of people is very powerful and the primary tool in the vilification of guns. The truth is that the Anti-2nd Radicals completely understand this too. They just choose to ignore it while they laugh and continue to play their strategic game of "Gotcha." We do a pretty good job holding them to account on their chosen talking points by countering with things like "A gun can't pull it's own trigger," but we can do much better. We can start by putting the focus on things that are at the cause of the senseless killings rather than being in the defensive position every time a Radical uses rhetoric to demonize guns.

It is clear to most logical thinking people that we have a problem in this country with mentally insane people, very angry people, gang violence and religious extremists that want to kill us. It's interesting how some of our fellow Americans refuse to acknowledge this. They may acknowledge it but certainly won't admit to it and definitely won't speak of it in public. In these times, we need to protect

130

ourselves. Not only from people that can physically harm us but also from people who are out to destroy our rights. To see the rhetoric and attacks against the idea of self-defense is astonishing. It's surprising that people can look reality in the face and deny it. We have the right to protect ourselves against people that seek to do us harm yet there are those among us who fight hard on a daily basis to eliminate that right. This doesn't make sense until you start to understand how the Anti-Gunner and the Anti-2nd Amendment Radicals think.

Why do some people continue to fight against the idea of self-preservation? Fear is the main driver for Anti-Gunners. They have been programmed for so long to believe that deaths are caused, not by people but by guns. There is a delusional thought process that concludes that if guns are eliminated, maniacs won't be able to kill. It's true, they actually believe this. Those who are able to break through the delusion yet still support the anti-gun agenda do not admit to the reality and change course because the actual causes of the problem are much bigger and may never be resolved. Ignorance can be your best friend when you are overtaken by fear and have no way to actually fix the problem.

It's not only disturbing to see this ignorance in our society but it's also dangerous. It's dangerous to us and it's dangerous to future generations. The good news is that much of the liberal anti-gun ideology is not the ideology of most Americans despite what President Obama, Hillary Clinton and the media would like you to believe. When President Obama makes comments that imply most Americans want strict gun laws because the current laws do not reflect who we are as a people, I have to sit back and absorb the arrogance. The implication that *he* knows "who we are" is a blatant slap in the face to the millions of Americans who see right through the broken and corrupt liberal ideology.

To garner support for gun restrictions from the public, many anti-gun politicians will use the argument that we should do anything we can to reduce "gun violence" even if it saves only one life. What that really means is they will use guilt to enforce more restrictions on law abiding gun owners. Who wouldn't want to save a life? I would and I'm sure most would agree, but at what expense? Making everyone helpless or rendering firearms useless when they are most needed? The "save one life" argument is invalid and those using it hope you don't call them on it. Saving one life is not worth losing many and that is exactly what happens every time someone is killed in an area where they are not allowed to defend themselves or their firearms are disassembled and locked away in their own home because they fear becoming a felon for having it ready in case of an emergency.

In order to support gun control you must first believe the following:

1. Government will always protect your freedoms.

All we have to do to destroy this illogical thinking is look at all the Countries that stole the freedom of their people immediately after controlling their use of guns.

- 1911, Turkey enacted gun control and soon after killed 1.5 million Armenians
- 1929, The Soviet Union enacted gun control and over the next 24 years killed approximately 20 million who opposed government policy.
- 1935, China enacted gun control and killed 20 million political dissidents within 17 years.
- 1938, Germany enacted gun control and killed 13 million Jews in the 7 years that followed.
- 1956, Cambodia enacted gun control and killed 1 million people by 1977

- 1964, Guatemala enacted gun control and killed 100,000 Mayan Indians by 1981
- 1970, Uganda enacted gun control and by 1979 300,000 Christians were killed.

2. You or your loved ones will never be attacked and/or your life threatened.

Tell that to the 1,165,383 people who (in the year 2014 alone) were the victims of violent crimes -FBI 2014 Crime Statistics, released September 28, 2015

3. If guns are removed from society we will be safe.

This belief must be preceded by the belief that it is actually possible to remove all guns from society. There are approximately 8.9 guns per every 10 people in America. Removing them will never happen. Restrictions will only affect law-abiding citizens and encourage the criminals, putting good people in more danger.

4. The mental instability of the perpetrator is of much less a concern than the gun.

This is a thought process that has been adopted only because there has yet to be any real effort to handle the issue of detecting mental illness, drug use (legal and illegal) and maniacal behavior before it results in the death of innocent people in America.

5. If I'm ever in danger, all I have to do is dial 911

The average response time of local police is 10 minutes. In Detroit, Michigan the quickest response time is 31 minutes, the average is 58 minutes and it may take as long as 115 minutes for a police officer to arrive on the scene. A mugging at knife-point takes 10 seconds *if* you don't resist.

Good Gun Bad Guy

The idea that some people denounce guns and believe that we don't need them is a dangerous thought. To know that someone could break into your home and harm your family and still believe that being unarmed and helpless is a good position to be in is a perfect example of the illogical thinking that comes from the anti-gun crowd. I've heard people say, *"I have a nine iron and my cell phone."* As if that will protect you against a maniac with a gun. I would suggest they never bring a nine iron to a gunfight, but not everyone takes my advice.

The gun owners in America don't ask for much with respect to this debate. All we ask is that when you look at the question of whether or not guns are a good thing to have, you look at it with a very simple and logical approach. If a Bad Guy points a gun in your face, would it be a good idea for you to have one too? The idea that some people can ignore the reality of violent crime in order to support the anti-2nd Amendment agenda is beyond comprehension to many people. I used to scratch my head wondering how they are able to concoct such a notion. To even begin to understand this thought process, we have to assume that the Anti-2nd Radical believes that with enough effort they will be able to rid our society of all guns.

This idea is similar to the idea that we can remove drugs or alcohol. We had Prohibition. Did that work? No, it pushed alcohol underground, spawned a black market and led to the growth of urban crime organizations. It's interesting to see how prohibition ended with President Franklin Roosevelt signing into law the Cullen–Harrison Act, legalizing beer and wine. This happened after it lost supporters and tax revenue as the years went on. The war on drugs started in 1971 and has since turned pot-smokers into felons, incarcerated drug users sometimes longer than sex offenders and has created an epidemic of prescription drug use which in many cases leads to heroin and other dangerous drugs.

The war on drugs is now changing direction. Marijuana is now legal in some states but only after the Global Commission on Drug Policy released a critical report stating that: *"The global war on drugs has failed, with devastating consequences for individuals and societies around the world."* The war on guns seems similar in many ways. It's clear that to have a war on anything you need to have two sides. As soon as the "war" doesn't benefit the "pro-war" side, it ends. It would be my hypothesis that as soon as enough Anti-2nd Radicals experience the negative effects of the "war on guns", they too will reverse course.

Good Gun Bad Guy

6. GUN FREE ZONES

"An armed society is a polite society. Manners are good when one may have to back up his acts with his life."

-Robert A. Heinlein

Gun Free Zones are an invitation for killers to commit heinous crimes. We all know that. It only takes a tiny bit of logic to understand this, but let's examine the GFZ in detail.

Everyone in a GFZ is helpless and unarmed but the worst part is the public announcement by posting a sign that reads:

"This is a gun free zone."

If you were to visit Earth from another planet and came upon one of these signs you would have to think the people were absolutely insane. No matter how many cute words and complex justifications liberals use to defend these idiotic killing zones, it never adds up. It never will because Gun Free Zones are illogical. The reason they are still supported amidst the countless data showing they don't work is because the Anti-2nd Radicals have been relentless in putting the focus on the gun while disregarding and refusing to talk about the zone or the killer. Pro-gunners have only recently been proactive in shining a spotlight on the GFZ. The media is still unwilling to even entertain the thought that maybe they're a bad idea.

The Gun-Free School Zones Act (GFSZA) is a federal United States law that prohibits any unauthorized individual from knowingly possessing a firearm at a place that the individual knows, or has reasonable cause to believe, is a school zone as defined by 18 U.S.C. § 921(a)(25). Such a firearm has to move in or affect interstate or foreign commerce for the ban to be effective.

It was introduced in the U.S. Senate in October 1990 by Joseph R. Biden and signed into law in November 1990 by George H. W. Bush.

The Gun-Free School Zones Act of 1990 was originally passed as section 1702 of the Crime Control Act of 1990.

By creating a GFZ we are letting everyone know that if you want to kill people with zero opposition, you've come to the right place. If you are a crazed lunatic, you can shoot the place up and there will be no one inside or on the premises equipped to defend themselves. At least until the cops arrive with guns, but that could take between 5-15 minutes. The idea behind the Gun Free Zone was most likely that the Bad Guys would be scared of the penalty and would not bring a firearm onto the property. Now let me ask you, if someone is intent on killing people does it make sense to believe that the penalty for possessing a gun in a restricted area would change their mind? If they're willing to commit the worst possible crime–Murder, why would they be concerned with breaking a GFSZ law? What in the world were our lawmakers thinking when they put this one together and why after all the deaths in Gun Free Zones since, has the law not been reversed or security put in place to counter the horrible effects of GFZ's?

Whether or not Gun Free Zones are target locations for indiscriminate killers has long been a topic of debate. Pro-Gunners demand that the facts and numbers be taken into consideration while

Anti-Gunners hold onto the belief that GFZ's make people safer.

The Stanford Geospatial Center and Stanford Libraries did a study called The Stanford Mass Shootings of America (Stanford MSA). The project began in 2012 in reaction to the Sandy Hook mass shooting and contained data from as far back as 1996. The Stanford MSA is an ongoing study and information discussed here is primarily from the time between 2002 and 2015. The study defined a mass shooting as a shooting of (3) or more victims not including the shooter and not including gang or drug related shootings.

Since 2002 the study reports 153 incidents, 54 of which involved the random targeting of victims who were not related to or adversaries of the shooter. In other words, 35 percent of these attacks could be considered "random acts of violence." In 37 of the 54 incidents, Gun Free Zones were chosen as the locations to carry out these acts. Only 17 of the 54 incidents were in areas where guns were legally allowed. This equates to 69% of the attacks taking place in Gun Free Zones. Another interesting piece of information is the fact that 29% of the attacks where citizens where allowed to carry a firearm were stopped or slowed down by a Good Guy with a gun. The math just does not work in favor of the anti-gun agenda and they hate that.

This information certainly doesn't surprise Pro-Gunners but the idea that data like this can be overlooked or disregarded in the attempt to further an anti-gun agenda is dangerous to society. The question that confuses most people is; why when in the face of this reality and given the option of being armed or unarmed against a potential killer some would choose to be unarmed? It wouldn't even be so bad if some chose to be a victim of violence, but to put others in the same helpless position is destructive and selfish.

Gun Free School Zones make our kids defenseless but our

politicians double down because it supports their agenda, of condemning the gun and arguably gaining control over the people. The liberal gun-grabbers know that the Bad Guys will never give up their guns. So why do they continue to double down on laws and restrictions when they know the restrictions will only affect the Good Guys? Here's why. You ready? They really want to disarm the law abiding gun owners because they know that lawful gun owners are the *real* opposition to their fantasyland society. The Constitution-loving Conservatives are the ones that will put a damper on their left-wing liberal agenda and they know it. The truth is that in any of these school shootings, had there been a Good Guy with a gun nearby, the children would have had a much better chance of survival. Without some means of stopping the madman, he will go as long as he wants or until his ammo runs out.

The Sandy Hook shooting is actually an argument for more gun protection, not restrictions. How "Moms Demand Action" think they are able to use it as a tool to restrict gun ownership defies all logic and morals. We need to protect our kids, not make them more vulnerable. What groups like "Moms Demand" and "Everytown" are doing is irresponsible, dangerous and borderline criminal. Our children need and count on us to protect them. These anti-gun, 2nd amendment hating groups are putting our kids in danger by making them helpless. Sandy Hook should have been a wake-up call for us to get tough against violent criminals. What these groups are doing is shameful and reprehensible. Here's what happened on that horrible day. You decide if a Good Guy with a gun would have saved lives.

- Sometime before 9:30 am investigators believe Adam Lanza, 20, killed his mother, Nancy Lanza.
- Lanza left the house wearing black fatigues and a military vest in possession of a semi-automatic rifle and two pistols.

(3) guns total. He went to the elementary school. This, according to a law enforcement official.

- 700 students were on the premises and classes had already begun.

- The school had recently installed a new security system that required visitors to be visibly identified and buzzed in. Principal, Dawn Lafferty Hochsprung, ordered this part of the security system. The door was locked before Lanza arrived.

- Authorities say Lanza used the rifle to shoot an entrance into the building.

- Hochsprung heard loud pops. She, school psychologist Mary Sherlach and Vice Principal Natalie Hammond went out to investigate. Hammond returned from the hallway wounded. Hochsprung and Sherlach did not return.

- At about 9:30 a.m., while loudspeaker announcements were being made, shots were heard throughout the school.

- Teachers directed students into closets and bathrooms as soon as the shots were heard.

- Lanza made his way toward two classrooms-one kindergarten class and one first grade class.

- Lauren Rousseau was a substitute teacher for the kindergarten class. Lanza shot all 14 students in that classroom.

- Victoria Soto was the first grade teacher in the other classroom. When she heard the gunshots she moved her first-grade students away from the door. According to the father of a surviving student, Lanza burst in and shot her. Six students were killed in that classroom.

- By the time police arrived on the scene and approached Lanza he had already killed 20 students, 6 adults and himself.

Let me be perfectly clear. When my family and I heard about this senseless act of violence perpetrated on these innocent children and teachers we were saddened to the core. I don't think I can even imagine what it would be like to lose a child. I hope all the surviving family members will somehow find peace.

What do you think would have been the outcome, had there been an armed guard at the door to greet Lanza?

I don't like when situations like this are used for political purposes and I was even hesitant to write about it. But because of the seriousness and danger Gun Free Zones create, I felt it would be responsible to show this particular mass killing in the hopes of shedding light on the situation and exposing the lies and risks that are inherent in these dangerous GFZ's. Some people say that the Sandy Hook shooting was all a complete hoax to further the gun-restricting agenda. That is for you to decide, but even if it was, this situation is not an argument for more Gun Free Zones or more gun restrictions. This is an argument for armed security guards in our schools and/or the ability for licensed concealed-carry staff members to be allowed the right to protect themselves and our children.

Whether those guards are police officers or retired veterans, our schools would be a much safer place with them around. Lanza or any other killer would have been taken out long before they could ever create this much destruction had someone been prepared and allowed to do the right thing. GFZ's and the false narrative that "they save lives" need to be stopped and the people who support the implementation of these zones into our society need to be aware of the dangerous environment they are creating. They need to be held accountable. We conscientious, caring Americans never want to see this happen again.

The solution is to remove the Gun Free Zones and allow

Constitutional carry. The accusation and false narrative from the Anti-2nd Radicals is that Pro-Gunners want to make it mandatory that *all* the teachers be armed. They then claim that this will lead to many accidents, teachers being overpowered by students and guns getting into the wrong hands. This is not the position of Pro-Gunners but rather another visual, imagery tactic by the anti-gun left. Responsible gun owners know that not all people are equipped or inclined to carry a firearm. The Anti-2nd Radicals spread the narrative of students killing their teachers in the classroom because of a bad grade and many other fairytales that evoke reactive fearful responses from people who buy into the rhetoric. The first misleading piece of their accusation is that Pro-Gunners want everyone to be armed. This is simply not true and another dishonest and misleading tool in their false narrative. What many responsible gun owners want is for staff members that are properly trained and inclined to carry a firearm be allowed to do so.

Putting guns in the hands of people that are not equipped for the job would be irresponsible. But the Anti-2nd Radicals are not honest with their narrative and strive only to paint the ugliest possible picture. Logic and data tells us that in a society where deadly crimes occur, it is imperative that we protect ourselves because the cops are never there in time. We are doing the exact opposite in the areas where we have the most precious lives – our schools. It doesn't take a team of rocket scientists to figure this one out. It only takes minimal logic to understand that Gun Free Zones equal death to innocent people. Gun Free Zones equal a safe haven for the Bad Guys to do their dirty work. Gun Free Zones must be stopped and anyone that supports them must be held to account.

There is a bit of hope amidst all the illogic that fuels Gun Free Zones. April 11th, 2016 was a good day for freedom and creating a safer environment for our kids when Kingsburg Joint Union High School District's board voted in favor of a policy that would allow

143

staff members to carry concealed on campus. The vote was unanimous and the policy allows a limited number of trained teachers and staff members to protect the children should a would-be attacker attempt to do them harm.

The new policy allows up to five teachers and staff at a time to be armed. The policy also keeps the concealed-carriers anonymous for their protection. Superintendent Morris said, "I am a proponent of the 2nd Amendment, and I'm also the biggest proponent of protecting the kids."

When referring to the Sandy Hook killings in 2012, Kingsburg police Chief Neil Dadian who supports the school district's new policy said, *"Imagine if one of those teachers was also armed. They could have stopped that. ... The loss of life would've been much less. My opinion? If a staff member wants to put themselves at risk like that, I'm all for it. I think what they're doing is everything they possibly can to protect their students, and God bless them for that."*

Of course there was opposition from the anti-gun crowd and a woman, whose grandchildren attend schools in the district used typical rhetoric when she referred to the policy as being akin to measures out of the "wild west." The woman was also quoted by the Fresno Bee as saying, *"Now we're going to add something else for teachers to think about? Shooting people, really? That's a difficult thing for a police officer to do who's been trained to do this, and you have a split second to decide if you should kill this person or not. I wouldn't want that responsibility, and I wouldn't want it for our teachers."*

The unwillingness to take responsibility seems to be a common thread among Anti-Gunners. I often wonder if people think of the alternative when they say things like that. In other words, would it be better to be helpless? Is taking responsibility for defending yourself and the people around you so painful that you would rather be a

144

victim? It is this ignorance of the positive that allows people to stay focused only on the negative. A relentless and persistent search for anything that could go wrong, coupled with an avoidance of the potential for good, seems to be ingrained in the psyche of Anti-Gunners. They can't seem to break the chains of this mental barrier. If they did, they would have to admit that self-preservation is important and they have a responsibility to themselves, their families and the good people around them to do their part.

Schools are not the only places where anti-gun policies fester. How about military bases? You would think that the last place to make a Gun Free Zone would be a military base because the people are trained and would be the most suited to handle firearms. But no, gun-grabbers don't think like you and me. Fort Hood Military base in Texas became "Gun Free" in 1993 under Democrat President Bill Clinton (initiated in 1992 under George H.W. Bush by the Department of Defense), then a mass-killing occurs in 2009 by an Islamist killer named Nidal Malik Hasan. Hasan screamed "Allahu Akbar" as he killed Lt. Col. Juanita Warman, 55 of Havre de Grace, MD., Maj. Libardo Caraveo, 52 of Woodbridge, VA., Cpt. John P. Gaffaney, 54 of San Diego, CA., Cpt. Russell Seager, 41 of Racine, WI., Staff Sgt. Justin Decrow, 32 of Plymouth, IN., Sgt. Amy Krueger, 29 of Kiel, WI., Spc. Jason Hunt, 22 of Tillman, OK., Spc. Frederick Greene, 29 of Mountain City, TN., PFC Aaron Nemelka, 19 of West Jordan, UT., PFC Michael Pearson, 22 of Bolingbrook, IL., PFC Kham Xiong, 23 of St. Paul, MN., Pvt. Francheska Velez, 21, Chicago, IL., and Michael G. Cahill, Cameron of Texas. He also wounded more than 30 others and took the life of an unborn baby that Francheska Velez was carrying at the time.

Did this change the minds of anti-gun politicians? Of course it didn't. At that point you might start to think that maybe this whole Gun Free Zone thing is not such a great idea. What did they do? Nothing. Well, an attempt was made and legislation was introduced

145

to end the policy, but it was quickly shot down by the then Democrat controlled House. So, Fort Hood remained gun free. Well, maybe it was just a fluke. It could never happen again, right? At least not for a few years. On April 2nd, 2014 it happened again. A mentally ill Iraq war veteran opened fire on his unarmed fellow service members, killing Sgt. 1st Class Danny Ferguson, Staff Sgt. Carlos A. Lazaney-Rodriguez and Sgt. Timothy Owens and wounding 16 others before committing suicide. During the attack the fully capable yet disarmed soldiers were told to "shelter in place until police arrived." That was their only defense.

The law specifically stated: *"The authorization to carry firearms will be issued ONLY to qualified personnel when there is a reasonable expectation that life or Department of the Army assets will be jeopardized if firearms are not carried."* I guess two mass-killings are not "reasonable expectation." Now you're thinking, *"That's it; it can't possibly continue to be a Gun Free Zone after all this data showing the negative affects of this backward policy."* Well, guess again. Fort Hood remains a Gun Free Zone to this day. If you're outraged, you're not alone. Conservative people across the country cannot understand how otherwise logical people can support this type of thinking.

We know the dangers of GFZ's. It amazes me that the information falls on deaf ears. But when you stop to think about it, you realize that there is a reason the Anti-2nd Radicals choose ignorance over logic. There could be a couple of different reasons for the continued support of these killing zones. One, could be the idea that if guns were heavily restricted the government could take control over the people. The reason this would be attractive to some is that they believe this would create a safe society (Utopia). People always do what they think is best. I believe the intent of people is most always good. The idea that they would create GFZ's with intent of people getting killed is not believable. In reality, they probably mean well.

Anti-2nd Radicals could quite possibly believe that government control over the people is best to keep everyone safe and society under control. Or they simply could be so scared of guns that rather than learn about them and understand how they work, they choose to stick their head in the sand and ignore the facts. This concept is similar to a child who can't sleep at night because she is scared of the monster in her closet. What does she do? She pulls the blankets over her head and pretends the monster doesn't exist in the hopes that the big bad scary thing will just go away. In this case the scary things are guns. This is the mindset that we are allowing a seat at the negotiating table.

There is no logical reason that people should even entertain this type of debate but the anti-2nd amendment voice is loud regardless of the fact that their argument has no validity. As a matter of fact in most cases law-abiding gun owners take a defensive position when the anti-gun rhetoric begins. Responsible Americans need to be proactive rather than reactive on these matters. Pro-Gunners always seem to be "defending" their rights when they should be free to "exercise" them. The approach Pro-Gunners take in this debate is essential. By defending our rights and being reactive, we lose ground. By exercising our rights and being proactive we gain ground and move the ball forward.

Firearms are used for self-defense between 2.1 and 2.5 million times per year. In over 1.9 million of these cases, a handgun was used – From "Armed Resistance to Crime": The Prevalence and Nature of Self-Defense with a Gun. Published in the Northwestern University School of Law's Journal of Criminal Law and Criminology, 1995

John R Lott Jr., a leading gun researcher and author of the book

Good Gun Bad Guy

"More Guns, Less Crime" concluded that firearms are used sixty times more when protecting lives than when taking lives. What would happen to those numbers if good people weren't able to own guns but Bad Guys still did? You have to look no further than Gun Free Zones for the answer to that question.

On November 13th, 2015, 130 people were killed in strategically planned attacks by radical Islamic terrorists. The brutal assaults were perpetrated on innocent people in Paris France. The majority of the killings were done in a concert hall that held 1500 people. It is unclear exactly how many people were in the venue at the time of the attacks but some reports say it was a sold out show. Paris is very restrictive when it comes to gun laws and the ability of its people to carry in public for the purpose of self-defense. Remember the French do not have the right to bears arms like we do in the United States, therefore all the innocent victims in the attacks were unarmed, defenseless and helpless. All they could do was lie down on the floor and pray. Some begged for their lives and others "played dead." It took approximately 10 minutes for the terrorists to achieve their goal. My question is; what would the outcome have been if good people were armed?

In the State of Florida 1.3 million people are legally licensed to carry a gun. That is approximately 6.5% of the State's population. Had the Paris number of conceal-carriers been similar to Florida, 98 concert goers would have potentially been carrying. If in this hypothetical scenario, only 20% of those licensees were actually carrying at the time of the event, that would equate to approximately 20 people armed and able to defend themselves and others. Would the terrorists have been able to kill that many people if they had the opposition of 20 citizens defending and protecting themselves and those around them?

Many would think the concert-goers would have had a much

148

better chance of survival, had a reasonable percentage of them been armed.

Donald Trump said, *"Paris would have been much, much different if some victims had been packing."*

Former House Speaker Newt Gingrich said, *"Imagine a theater with ten or fifteen conceal-carry guns. Evil men have to be killed by good people."*

But of course there are those who find the idea of self-defense preposterous. Anti-2nd Radicals were anxious to get in front of cameras immediately after the killings to spread their misleading and dangerous ideas to as many people as possible. Fox 32 News from Chicago went to the streets to see what some Anti-Gunners thought about the Paris killings and the idea of good people being able to defend themselves.

"More guns in those type of situations lead to more tragedy" is what anti-gun activist Colleen Daily said, citing also that those who "fire back" have hit hundreds of people.

Another fearful Anti-Gunner was interviewed and said, *"If more people had guns, there probably would have been more bloodshed. Because in the confusion of the attack people would not have known who were the good guys or the bad guys."*

Really? Not know who the Bad Guys were? It takes a special kind of ignorance to make a statement like that.

When asked if he thought good people in the venue having guns would have made a difference, another denier said, *"No, I don't think it would have made any difference at all and I'm not a believer in the concept."*

Not a believer in the concept? Of what, guns being used to kill people or good people being able to defend themselves? Sometimes the illogic that comes from the Anti-2nd Amendment crowd is staggering. It's difficult for logical thinking people to make sense of it.

During the Fox broadcast they shared the opinions of some other Anti-Gunners. This is what one person had to say, *"France has good gun laws. They don't need every lunatic running around with a weapon like America does."*

Every lunatic running around with a weapon? The imagery here is crystal clear but I sometimes wonder if Anti-Gunners intend on creating this type of visual or if they have been so brainwashed to believe this rhetoric that they just can't help it. They obviously believe the things they say when they lash out against the idea of people defending themselves because you can see the passion when they speak. This is very real to them and they take the defenseless passive approach over the proactive "take control of the situation" kind of attitude when it comes to self-defense. Yes, they actually believe that during a mass killing it is better if the good people have no way to defend themselves. Somehow they think that being helpless is better. You can't make this stuff up. This is a result of consistent anti-gun marketing and powerful control over a group of very fearful people.

It seems that personality and character traits play a big role in a person's stance on guns and political positioning for that matter. It would otherwise be perfectly fine for someone to have these anti-gun views if they didn't try to push them on everyone else and change laws that affect the safety of others. It's ok for them to believe whatever they want in their own homes but when they try to inflict their fear (disguised as rules of moral conduct) on you, it's time to remind them of their position in the argument. It takes a certain level of arrogance when they tell you what you should or should not be allowed to do with respect to self-defense.

The Anti-2nd Radicals seem to forget that they haven't been invited to participate in the debate because the 2nd Amendment is non-negotiable. 2nd Amendment supporters will never sit down with them and try to come up with something that makes them happy. However, Anti-2nd Amendment Radicals still like to force their opinions on whoever is within earshot. This is not the case with Pro-gunners though. People who are pro-gun tend to keep their opinions to themselves in public forum. That is a respectable approach but some may argue that it is ineffective in the fight to defend the 2nd Amendment. That is starting to change as Pro-Gunners are becoming much bolder in their approach and public stance. We are starting to make our collective voice heard; and it is a powerful voice. I suspect the battle will heat up more before it settles down.

Good Gun Bad Guy

7. THE RESPONSIBILITY OF FREEDOM

I'm not asking for permission from the Government to keep and bear arms. My 2nd Amendment is a warning to the Government to remind them who they work for.

I started out as a kid who really wasn't interested in guns, even though there were guns in my house throughout my entire childhood. My Dad would show me his new pistols and I would watch him build muzzle loader replicas. I even went hunting with him a few times and shot at tin cans in the field down from the graveyard in Charlton, NY. I understood how important guns were to my Dad but they were not really my thing at the time. I was fascinated with guitar and that is all I thought about. Guns were just something my father did and I sometimes participated.

As time went on into my twenties I started to develop a feeling of disdain toward guns because I started to link them to death, destruction and all the violence and mayhem the media surrounded them with. My feelings toward guns went from a general lack of interest to a strong fear and contempt. I became very influenced by the anti-gun rhetoric, despite the fact that I never had a single bad experience with guns. My Dad had died by that point so I didn't have him to help me through the misguided fear of guns. I went for a ride on the media crazy train. At the time, it felt right and seemed to

153

make sense. The media packages everything in a way that makes unsuspecting people feel stupid for *not* jumping on board with the anti-gun agenda.

Our beliefs are ingrained. They are our subconscious thought process. Our beliefs are a big part of who we are. They have a big role in defining our character. When we believe something, it is part of who we are as a person. Those beliefs are developed by consistent, repetitive experiences. Beliefs can also be developed by experiences we have when we are in a heightened emotional state. You may have a sight, scent, sound or even a song that reminds you of your childhood. It's most likely because when you experienced that particular thing, you were in a highly emotional state. It got anchored in your subconscious.

Repetition is a way to anchor a belief when heightened emotional states are not necessarily an option. The media and marketing companies know this so they use repetition to convince you of things they want you to believe. It may be something as harmless as getting you to switch deodorant or as dangerous and deceiving as convincing you to fear and denounce guns.

As I started to collect more data on guns, I began to realize that the media was delivering false information and making it look like guns were the cause of everything bad in the world. Logically I knew that wasn't true because my Dad always had guns and nothing bad ever came from them. As a matter of fact my Dads guns brought us together and provided him with great pleasure.

The inevitable thought eventually occurred that if gun violence *was* as prominent in our society as the media made it out to be, it would only make sense to me that without having a gun, good people would be at risk. The anti-gun narrative started to have the opposite effect on me. The math was becoming very easy; if Bad Guys use guns to kill good people, then not having one to defend myself equaled helplessness. I wasn't sure how it was that I fell into the anti-gun media trap for a short time but reality was finally becoming clear. I know it makes complete sense that not having a gun when you need one puts you in a vulnerable position but my thought process during my twenties wouldn't let me see that logic. I explain this piece to illustrate what goes on in the minds of many Anti-Gunners. That simple logic is lost on them.

During my transition I had a very difficult conflict going on in my mind. The reactive feelings I had about guns were generally of a negative nature but the thought process told me that guns made logical sense. The conflict between my logical thought process and my internal belief process had an ongoing battle for a period of time but logic eventually prevailed when my wife and I were in a potentially dangerous situation. I finally decided that I would do whatever necessary to protect myself and my family. At that point I wanted to learn everything I could about guns. I was especially interested in handguns so I collected every piece of data I could get my hands on. As I got involved, the thing that was most surprising to me was the thoughtfulness of the people. The people who trained me and the fellow shooters at the range were very helpful and held me accountable to everything. They didn't let me get away with taking any shortcuts or avoiding any safety precautions. They told me what I was doing wrong with my stance, grip and breathing, talked to me in depth about the responsibilities that go along with carrying and countless other topics that I would have had to figure out or re-learn on my own. The picture Anti-2nd Radicals paint of responsible gun owners is the exact opposite of reality. The truth is, shooters and Pro-Gunners are some of the most respectable and responsible people I have ever met.

It's sad and disgusting that Anti-2nd Radicals will do and say whatever they think will cast the gun culture in a bad light. They do it

155

out of desperation and the need for control. When people are desperate they compromise their ethics because achieving the goal sometimes becomes more important than upholding morals, values or truth. Failure in achieving their agenda is the most devastating thing to them and when they're up against the wall, the claws come out. Right now they are up against the wall because they know no one is above the Constitution, even the President of the United States. Although anti-gun politicians like Barack Obama and Hillary Clinton portray themselves to be the ones who will save the world from the guns (they have demonized), they find it very difficult because the majority of Americans understand the importance of firearms in our culture. Historically, openly campaigning on an anti-gun platform has proven destructive for Presidential hopefuls.

As a gun owner, I know that guns provide protection, sport and even food but there is much more to owning guns that some will never understand. Mechanically they're are fascinating, the people are great and the entire culture is welcoming and fun. The politics are the twisted part of the whole thing. Being an avid gun owner and enthusiast, you can't help being aware of the political opposition. Most Americans understand why guns are so important to our culture and self-preservation, but what I've noticed about the people who tend to be anti-gun is that they have a different set of internal beliefs. I understand how beliefs play into the argument. It's very clear to me because I ran the gamut of emotion on the topic myself.

It became clear to me that the battle between Anti-Gunners and Pro-Gunners would go nowhere until we understood what they were thinking. By understanding them we are better equipped to counter the lies, anger and rhetoric that gets thrown in our direction. By understanding their fear and anger we may also be able to help them see the importance of self-defense and protecting the ones they care about while also helping them understand the responsibility we all have to uphold our freedom and defending the mission statement we all live by – The Constitution.

Luckily for us we have a set of guidelines that among other things, allows us the ability to protect ourselves against people that want to do us harm. That particular right is written in the 2nd Amendment of the Bill of Rights. When it comes to the Constitution and the Bill of Rights, it amazes me that there are actually people in this country, citizens of the United States who will fight tooth and nail against the Constitution. They will fight to destroy our beautiful mission statement.

Most businesses have a mission statement. It is a set of standards that the employees and officers live by. It is designed to guide the organization in a way that supports the company and the people in it. A mission statement sets the standard and overall moral path of the company. It is put in place to help people remember the goals and reason the company was created in the first place. Should people divert or stray from the mission statement, the guidelines therein define the parameters so the people can get themselves back on track.

Our Constitution serves as America's mission statement. It was designed with the same intent. Over 200 years ago a group of very smart men we call our "Founding Fathers" created the Constitution and the Bill of Rights with a focus on ethics, morals and an agreed upon set of guidelines. The group of men responsible for drafting the Constitution were Alexander Hamilton, James Madison, John Adams, Thomas Jefferson, Governeur Morris and others. It was compiled over approximately 100 days, was influenced by many people and was overseen by George Washington.

The most amazing thing about the Constitution was the foresight into the future these men had. Here we are, now in the future and we realize that if that document had not been created we would be in big trouble because those who wish to destroy our way of life would have very possibly been able to do just that by now. Luckily for us we have that document because if we didn't, we would be living in a very different world. Do you think we could write a document like that now? Could we write a mission statement for our country now with foresight 200-300 years into the future that would be able to serve future generations? Do we have the moral fortitude and ethical values to do that?

I'm not sure we have the ability to create a moral standard that would define what America is right now and what it should be in the future. Some might argue that because we have many cultures, religions and ideologies living together in America it would be impossible to agree on a set of beliefs and a standard to live by. Thankfully those standards have been created and designed in a way that is defended against opposition. In other words, those who want to destroy or dismantle our rights have no negotiating power. When it comes to the use and ownership of firearms, the 2nd Amendment to the Constitution spells it out very clearly. It reads:

"A well regulated Militia, being necessary to the security of a free State, the right of the people to keep and bear Arms, shall not be infringed."

- **A well regulated Militia:** A group of people organized, armed, trained and acting under a plan or set course of action. The Revolutionary War was partly comprised of these Militias in the overtaking of the British army. These were groups of individual men, not professional soldiers.

- **Being necessary to the security of a free State:** The recognition that there may come a time when the Militia will need to gain leverage over those who attempt to control the State and the people. The ability for the people to create a Militia was guaranteed early on to defend against a tyrannical government, should that government decide to take power over the very people who created it. Our Framers were aware of this possibility because they had just experienced and defeated the standing armies of England. Should the United States have standing armies, they would make sure the leverage against them would be available to the people should the armies begin to overtake the will of the people.

- **The right of the people to keep and bear arms:** Assuring that the people of the State will always have the right to own firearms for any and all purposes. Without this right, the ability to form an effective Militia would be impossible, as the militia is comprised of the people and their ability to re-gain leverage if necessary. Some Anti-2nd Amendment Radicals will argue that the right to keep and bear arms is reserved for militia members only and citizens should not have that right. That would benefit the Anti-2nd Radicals by ensuring militias never have the ability to form.

- **Shall not be infringed:** To infringe means to limit or undermine. At no time, for any reason will the right to bear arms be encroached, reduced, controlled or affected in any limiting way.

It is amazing that in America today, there is even an argument about what the 2nd Amendment means. It has been under constant attack and perverted in many ways as an attempt to reduce its effectiveness and credibility. There are those among us who want to see the 2nd Amendment repealed. They are a danger to the well-being of this country and the very freedoms we have built our society on. The claims and degradation have been preposterous but the 2nd Amendment, in its actual meaning has prevailed.

We have advanced technologically in ways that we would have never imagined even just fifty years ago. The question is; have our ethics kept up with the pace? Some might say we have regressed with respect to morals, ethics and responsibility for our actions. The good news is, we do in fact have the Constitution and thankfully so. Our Founding Fathers were smart enough and had a strong enough moral standard and foresight to create the document that would protect us from ourselves. They were helping us protect and defend ourselves from our worst enemy. You guessed it – us.

Upon the death of Supreme Court Justice, Antonin Scalia in early 2016, all eyes are on the Supreme Court to see how well the Constitution is defended. Of course the 2nd Amendment is of greatest concern because countless attempts have already been made to re-define it and render it useless by left-wing politicians. An interesting case came up immediately after Scalia's passing that threw out a decision by Massachusetts supreme Judicial Court. The case was Jamie Caetano v. Massachusetts and the Massachusetts Court determined that the stun-gun owned by Jamie Caetano was not protected by the 2nd Amendment.

Jamie Caetano had previously experienced multiple attacks by her ex-boyfriend and father of her two children. She decided she would not stand for the abuse anymore any threatened to defend herself with a stun-gun. Massachusetts decided that she could not do that and she (the victim) was arrested for defending herself. She faced a minimum fine of between $500 up to $1000 and 6 months to 2 and a half years in prison. You read that right. The victim was the criminal because the State Court determined that because stun-guns were not in existence when the 2nd Amendment was written, they were not protected.

The Massachusetts Court held that stun-guns were not protected by the 2nd Amendment because they "were not in common use at the time of the 2nd Amendment's enactment." To which the Supreme Court rejected as a direct affront to the landmark Heller v. District of Columbia case, which determined that the 2nd Amendment "extends to arms that were not in existence at the time of the founding." The Massachusetts Court's holding that stun-guns were "dangerous and unusual" devices in part because they were "a thoroughly modern invention" was also shot down. The Supreme Court said that "by equating 'unusual' with 'in common use at the time of the Second Amendment's enactment,' the Massachusetts court's second explanation is the same as the first; it is inconsistent with Heller v. District of Columbia for the same reason." Finally, the Massachusetts Court's holding that stun-guns were not "readily adaptable to use in the military" fell because "Heller v. District of Columbia rejected the proposition 'that only those weapons useful in warfare are protected.'"

This is a huge win, but to a battle that should have never needed to be fought. United States citizens should not have to defend themselves against States trying to obstruct the rights of it's own people. Any chance the Anti-2nd Amendment Radicals get to misuse power and set precedent to over-ride the right-to-defend, they will take advantage of. This case sparked a special interest for me; not because of the win, but because it reveals something much more interesting about the intent of those who try to disarm the population. For some it is clearly not about "the gun" and this case in particular exposes that. This case revealed the intent to disarm a citizen. Why? Because had the case been a victory for the State of Massachusetts, the precedent would have been set for other States to follow as they too determine self-defense illegal. The focus of Anti-Gunners appears to be on the fear and anger toward guns while the focus of Anti-2nd Amendment Radicals appears to be on disarming people regardless of the weapon they use. Anti-Gunners want to see guns go away because they are generally scared, uninformed and misled. Anti-2nd Amendment Radicals want all forms of self-defense to go away because they want control. In this case, they exposed themselves and got caught with their pants down.

I took this topic to my sounding board which consists of Pro-Gunners and Anti-Gunners. My friend Nate who always seems to favor the idea of an unarmed society had some very revealing things to say about the mindset of Anti-Gunners. The conversation went like this:

DW: Of course you know my position on self-defense, but I wanted to know what you think about stun-guns. You know, as a way for people to defend against an attacker.

Nate: I think it's a bad idea. There is no reason why people should have a thing like that.

DW: What about knives? Should they have the right to carry a knife?

Nate: Again, it's the same thing. We don't want people walking around with deadly weapons. At least I don't. You tell me when the last time was that you needed a knife to save your life from some deadly monster. It's unnecessary and barbaric.

DW: OK. So, what about a baseball bat? I know you think it could never happen, but let's just say hypothetically, I'm walking down the street and get attacked by some lunatic. Is it ok for me to bash his head in with my bat to save my own life?

Nate: That's ridiculous. You just don't understand. You're not getting it. The use of deadly weapons is not acceptable in a civilized society.

DW: So, it's not just about the gun?

Nate: No, it is about the gun. It's also about people taking the law into their own hands. The average person should not have access to deadly weapons. It puts everyone in danger.

DW: So if someone is attacked, they should call the cops and not defend themselves? You do know that it could take the cops 10 to 15 minutes just to get there, right?

Nate: Look, all I know is people do not need to carry their guns around with them. It's dangerous and just plain stupid. What are you guys so afraid of anyway?

As you can imagine, trying to help someone understand the importance of self-defense when they refuse to accept any reasonable argument can be very frustrating, but we continue to do the best we can. The refusal to acknowledge basic fundamentals of the argument shows a need to hold strong to their position, as if wavering or admitting to a contradicting belief would somehow damage them in some way. I will get into this more in the "I'm right, you're wrong" chapter and explore why some people vehemently hold onto their beliefs amidst consistent contradicting data.

A gun is an inanimate object. It is a series of components designed by man with the purposeful intent to expel a projectile. How did we manage to put the focus on the device and take it off the man who uses it with ill-intent? We have a responsibility to our families, our communities and our Constitution. Part of that responsibility includes holding people to account for their actions. We have a party in our government that clearly favors criminals over law-abiding citizens and makes their message clear by demonizing the gun and defending the law-breakers. You'll see this every time a maniac shoots up a school. But what happens when the Anti-

Good Gun Bad Guy

Gunners *can't* blame the gun?

Take for instance the Michael Brown shooting on August 9th, 2014 in Ferguson, Missouri. In this case it would have been politically damaging to the Democratic party in general if they sided publicly with Officer Darren Wilson because it would have ultimately reflected in a loss of black votes. They also couldn't blame the gun because it was in the hands of a cop and that would destroy their whole "cops are the only ones who should carry guns" narrative. That narrative is important to note here because they use it to justify gun restrictions on American citizens. So if they couldn't blame the criminal (who by the way was at fault according to the forensic evidence and the decision of the jury) and they couldn't blame the gun, then who could they blame? Of course, the police department and the way they mistreat black people. Makes sense right? If you need the black vote more than the respect of your own police department you would point the finger at the cop and perpetuate the racial divide in America. The votes are what keep parties in office, the police department is a controlled government entity.

Just think about how future events would have played out through 2014 and 2015 had our President done the right thing by defending the police department and condemned the criminal in this particular case. It is the contention of most Americans that had the criminal activity been condemned, the senseless vengeful killings of police officers that followed would not have happened. As the "hands up don't shoot" and later the "black lives matter" movement gained momentum without a word of condemnation from President Obama, amidst countless destructive rallies and protests, our police officers were put in grave danger very quickly. A big part of the problem is that people don't always stop to hypothesize the potential effects of their decisions. Those decisions affect us all and we have a responsibility to hold the perpetrators accountable, even, and sometimes especially our government officials.

164

When it comes to gun restrictions (which by the way only affect law-abiding citizens), Gun Free Zones and the general narrative that guns are bad and gun owners worse; we Americans have a responsibility. We as gun owners have a responsibility to look into the future and hypothesize the potential outcomes if we don't act. It is my belief that many gun owners are guilty of assuming the latest restriction du jour won't be so bad because *"it's just a small item that doesn't have much impact on my rights."* What we don't always recognize is the accumulative affect those small restrictions have. The perpetrators slowly strangle the 2nd Amendment with these small restrictions. The NRA has been our saving grace because the organization relentlessly fights at every step of the way. The shame is in the fact that the gun grabbers have the NRA so preoccupied with defending our rights that it can't put more effort into proactive events and causes. What kind of results could be achieved if it weren't bogged down in court all the time defending us against tyrants and fear mongers?

All we have to do to see the negative effects of irresponsible gun restrictions is look at other countries and regions of the world that take away the ability of people to defend themselves. It's amazing that evidence of government control over the people can be so obvious and destructive, yet the Anti-2nd Radicals still have an audience. A perfect example would be the multiple attacks on citizens in Paris, France.

Immediately after the November 13th, 2015 mass terrorist attacks in Paris, France, "Moms Demand Action" wanted to convince the world that guns were the cause while simultaneously linking the issue to "gun violence" in America. They couldn't even wait a day to show respect for the families of the lost victims. This is an example of an ideologically fueled agenda trumping human ethics. But in their attempt to vilify guns they made a mistake and showed how gun control makes good people defenseless while empowering the killers.

The "Moms Demand" group shared an article by the Daily Beast which explained how illegal guns flow from Eastern Europe into France. The article went on to talk about how gun trafficking is big business in that region and local authorities can't do much about it. It was also noted in the article that despite the French government's attempts at confiscating illegal guns, they still enter France and the rate at which they enter increases over 10% per year. The French government has made guns virtually off limits to its citizens and the terrorists are fully aware of this.

So while "Moms Demand" wants to put the fear of guns in the hearts of Americans by posting the article, the group in fact showed everyone how dangerous it is when people are unarmed and helpless against terrorists with firepower. They were also successful in showing everyone that gun restrictions do nothing to prevent illegal guns from entering the country, yet do everything to empower killers.

Don't take my word for it. Jesse Hughes, Frontman for the band Eagles of Death Metal had a first-hand experience of the deadly attack. He witnessed it from the stage that night. While holding back tears and barely able to compose himself as he recounted the event, Jesse said the following in an interview with a French reporter:

"Gun control kinda' doesn't have anything to do with it but if you want to bring it up, I'll ask you; did your French gun control stop a single fucking person from dying at the Bataclan? And if anyone can answer yes, I'd like to here it, because I don't think so. I think the only thing that stopped it was some of the bravest men that I have ever seen in my life charging head first into the face of death with their firearms. Maybe, I know people will disagree with me but it just seems like God made men and women and that night guns made them equal. I hate it that it's that way. I think the only way my mind has been changed is maybe that until

nobody has guns, everybody has to have them."

During the 2008-2016 Obama administration, gun owners have had to fight relentlessly just to preserve their rights. The constant barrage of restrictions and new rules of gun ownership have caused Americans to lose trust in Government, the Democrat party and more specifically Barack Obama himself. The anti-gun rhetoric coming from this President has been excessive. Every opportunity to politicize killings and violence with the intent to demonize guns and gun owners has been used. Some even call him "the most anti-gun President in history." By the time I write this we are nearing the end of the 2nd Obama term and we have learned how important it is to support the NRA and fight every battle with everything we have. We now understand that trusting anti-gun politicians is not an option and negotiating with our 2nd Amendment will never benefit us. So we don't.

It is our duty to keep dangerous politicians out of office but if they do get in, we must then keep them in line and make sure they remember who they work for. Although it can be daunting and it may feel like we are always losing, the fight to defend the rights of the people actually does pays off. There have been some substantial wins in the fight against Anti-2nd Amendment Radicals. Here are a few.

WIN!

In November 2015 the U.S. Court of Appeals for the D.C. Circuit issued a win against over-reaching government. The decision struck down four provisions of D.C. firearms law and handed justice to law abiding gun owners of Washington D.C.

In the *Heller v. District of Columbia* lawsuit, the 4 key provisions that were struck down are:

- The court overturned the limitation on registration of one handgun per month.

- The court struck down the three-year re-registration requirement, which imposed a never-ending burden on gun owners in the District.

- The court invalidated the requirement that the registrant physically bring the firearm to police headquarters to register it.

- The court struck down the requirement that applicants pass a test on D.C. gun laws, citing the lack of any public safety benefit.

Chris W. Cox, NRA-ILA Executive Director said, *"Today's ruling is a substantive win for the Second Amendment and the residents of our nation's capital."*

"For too long, the D.C. government has violated the constitutional rights of law-abiding citizens. The city has among the most restrictive gun laws in the nation; and yet one of the highest crime rates. This opinion makes it a little easier for lawful D.C. residents to own firearms for self-defense."

Dick Heller-Plaintiff in the historic 12 year case said, *"We still have to be registered and fingerprinted, so the worst part is we will still be treated like criminals, but the criminals won't be standing in line to get in."* He also said. *"On the positive side, the big win is you do not have to re-register your firearm every three years, and accidentally become a paper criminal by forgetting. Number two would be the one-gun-a-month restriction is now gone."*

WIN!

In 2014 in a 2-1 decision, the Ninth U.S. Circuit Court of Appeals in San Francisco ruled that by requiring citizens to prove "good cause" — rather than just the right to self-defense — in order to obtain a concealed weapons permit, San Diego County is in direct violation of the U.S. Constitution. If the decision stands, the permit system for the entire state of California would be invalidated – The Washington Post reported.

Judge Diarmuid O'Scannlain said, *"The right to bear arms includes the right to carry an operable firearm outside the home for the lawful purpose of self-defense."*

WIN!

In February 2015 in the Fredric Russell Mance, Jr. et al. v. (Attorney General) Eric H. Holder, Jr. and (Bureau of Alcohol, Tobacco, Firearms and Explosives Director) suit, Judge Reed O'Connor struck down a longstanding federal ban on interstate handgun sales. Determining the ban to be "unconstitutional".

B. Todd Jones, argued that the ban violated both the Second Amendment and the Due Process Clause of the Fifth Amendment. The defendants failed to proved that the law was "narrowly tailored" to achieve the desired legislative effect — presumably, public safety — with minimum impingement on individual liberties guaranteed by the Constitution.

Judge O'Connor wrote in his decision, *"Defendants failed to provide reasonably current figures to show the federal interstate handgun sale ban is narrowly tailored."*

The court also ruled that the law, had to withstand "strict scrutiny," but failed to hold up even under an "intermediate scrutiny test" because of its impact on constitutionally protected freedoms. Therefore, the ruling stated that the effect of the law was to impact liberty without achieving the "Government's stated goal" of improved public safety- the Firearms Policy Coalition reported.

Another win for the Good Guys!

WIN!

In July 2015 gun-nosy Florida doctors suffered a slap in the face when the U.S. Court of Appeals for the Eleventh Circuit upheld Florida's Firearm Owners' Privacy Act again. The law was passed after ongoing harassment about gun ownership and denial of service for gun owners came to a head. After constant interrogation by doctors, the law was passed. The plaintiffs and gun control advocates were not happy with the loss.

The appellate court stated, *"The essence of the Act is simple: medical practitioners should not record information or inquire about patients' firearm-ownership status when doing so is not necessary to providing the patient with good medical care."*

The Act *"protects a patient's ability to receive effective medical treatment without compromising the patient's privacy with regard to matters unrelated to healthcare."*

The New York Times was angrily quoted as stating, *"Censorship in Your Doctor's Office."*

A Florida physician's group called the decision "egregious" and "dangerous" and claimed it would silence "life-saving conversations."

What it really sounds like is the 4th Amendment flexing its

muscles and the people of America saying, *"Mind your own damn business."*

WIN!

In February, 2016 a three-judge panel of the U.S. Court of appeals for the 4th Circuit decided that a ban on semi-automatic firearms and so-called "high capacity" magazines previously under ban by Maryland's Firearm Safety Act was a violation to the 2nd Amendment.

Chris W. Cox, executive director of the National Rifle Association's Institute for Legislative Action, called this decision *"an important victory for the Second Amendment."*

Cox also said, *"Maryland's ban on commonly owned firearms and magazines clearly violates our fundamental, individual right to keep and bear arms for self-defense. The highest level of judicial scrutiny should apply when governments try to restrict our Second Amendment freedoms."*

There is a silver lining to what feels like a constant battle against a barrage of angry Antis trying to destroy our rights. The good news is the fact that we do have "wins". Sometimes those wins are quite substantial because they set a strong precedent for future attacks on the 2nd Amendment.

We enjoy our wins but we also know that with a win comes the increased ability to protect ourselves from people who are on a mission that results in the loss of human life. Not only are we dealing with the thought process of Anti-2nd Radicals, we are also simultaneously trying to defend ourselves from those who actually want to kill us. What is it about the minds of people who don't believe it's wrong to take the life of another person? Do we really have cold-blooded killers walking among us? Of course we like to disregard this fact because facing it means we must do something about it.

Allowing those who fear guns the ability to put us all in danger by imposing restrictions is irresponsible on our part. We, the responsible gun owners, have a duty to protect ourselves and the ones we love from evil, delusional or dangerous people. Although we shouldn't have to, the fact remains that we also have the responsibility to defend ourselves from the people who think it's best that we all be unarmed. In the process, we are also defending those people from their own demise, whether they know it or not. Compromising with our safety by accommodating fearful, ill-informed people is not an option. We don't want to find ourselves in a position where we are forced to say, "I told you so." So our "wins" are important to the safety of everyone.

Understanding the thought process of those who want to destroy our rights is as important as understand the thought process of a killer. Although rational thinking people may never truly know or understand what causes a killer to justify his actions, there have been many attempts to look into the minds of these deranged people.

Let's look at what goes on in the mind of a killer as best we can. Here is a guy that has no problem violating you for his own benefit. How does he justify it? What does he have to say in his thought process that makes it ok to kill you? There have been a number of studies and interviews with criminals. The James Broadnax jail interview brings to light some of the disturbing thought process that goes on in the minds of killers. Although most people will never truly understand how they justify their hideous actions; interviews with killers can give the clearest possible view of the thought process behind their murders. The full-length interview with Broadnax can be found online and I urge you to watch it if you dare.

By carefully studying this killer in particular, I found some interesting things. In the James Broadnax interview, the most disturbing human trait was his complete lack of remorse for what he did. There was no sense of wrong-doing. He seemed to have found a way to completely justify taking innocent life and destroying families. This was a bit confusing because contrary to his actions he also expressed love for his own family when he mentioned his mother and others in the interview. He made it a point to demand that the interviewers make sure his mother got his message. So a sense of love for his own family, yet complete disregard for another man's family was very clear.

Coupled with a disregard for human life he also showed a complete lack of accountability for what he did, going as far as blaming the gun for his actions. This seems to be a common thread with killers like this. They always blame someone or something else; whether it be the victim, someone who encouraged their actions, society and their position in it or any number of things. In an attempt to avoid the consequences of his actions, he challenged the cops and judge by saying he would kill more people in jail, if they didn't give him the death penalty. This part was interesting and displayed another example of him not being willing to take responsibility for what he did by living out his life in jail. He seemed to prefer the idea of being able to take the easier route, death.

At one point in the interview Broadnax said, *"Only God can judge me."* The interviewer responded by asking how he thought he would be judged and Broadnax replied by saying, *"Fuck him too."* So it seemed that a strong defiance would appear at the mere presence of opposition, even when the opposition was simply hypothetical. It also showed how easily he could turn on the one entity that he just seconds before authorized to morally judge him – God. Somehow in the minds of this killer and others there also appears to be a sense of

173

entitlement to things that don't belong to them. When asked about his intent in the crime that ended the lives of innocent people, Broadnax said he did it for the money, car and whatever else came with it.

What has to happen in the mind of a person who decides to use a weapon to hurt people? Many of us will never really understand this because it seems to be a dysfunctional thought process inaccessible to those who value human life. In other words, in order to truly understand it, we would have to own the same thoughts and feelings. So the best we can do is take data from documented studies and hypothesize based on the information we have.

It appears that a blocking of emotion and the lack of value for human life is a necessary strategy among many of these killers. Their strong sense of defiance and avoidance of personal responsibility are used to justify their actions. We could talk about what causes these traits and characteristics in a person and it would probably lead to poor family upbringing, poor choice in role models, an emboldened sense of entitlement, or any number of things. The fact is it would take generations to even begin making changes in the ethics and morals of humanity. I also understand that in the present time, there is a need and responsibility to protect ourselves until we reach that higher moral ground.

Many who push for gun-restrictions do not recognize the reality that maniacs don't have the same internal boundaries as you and I. It's easy to conceptualize a safe, killer-free environment when you are working with a moral standard that holds value for human life. It's also easy to believe that people will do the "right" thing if given trust and opportunities. That has been proven to not work. Instead, by trying to grasp what goes on in the minds of killers, we are more likely to understand the dangers we potentially face on a daily basis. A killer's mind is not changed by stricter gun-laws and they will not

174

magically value life just because we feel sorry for them. Those who recognize this reality have a duty to help others see it too. I've said it before and it is worth repeating; as destructive as the Anti-Gunner's policy ideas can be, I believe they most often pursue their goals with good intentions. They believe their anti-gun stance is a good thing because they want to believe people are good. I also believe they have been hijacked of their sense of reality when it comes to the actual safety issues we face by living in a society that includes multiple cultures, religions, ideologies and moral standards. As for the Anti-2nd Amendment Radicals, I believe they want nothing more than control based on their actions and strategic political moves.

For us as Americans (and humans for that matter) to actively pursue disarmament we are creating an environment where the Bad Guys are in charge. Often times the excuse falls within the narrative of "safety for the people," which is just another name for cowering and giving in to those who choose not to live by a high moral standard. We need to recognize that in societies like ours there will be dangerous people, selfish people and delusional people. If common sense does not come to the surface with respect to safety, we could be handing the jail-cell keys to the criminals.

Good Gun Bad Guy

8. LIES, LIES AND MORE LIES

The truth is, more people are showing an interest in firearms than the media would like us to believe. The problem is, the minority is much louder.

When I was a kid in the 70's and 80's we played with guns. Of course they were cap guns and BB guns. No one ever put an eye out and no one was ever traumatized by the sight of our cap guns. The times really weren't so different with respect to violence. I'll get into gun death statistics in a minute but not much has really changed. The topic of guns however, has become almost taboo and don't even think about giving your kid a BB gun for Christmas anymore. If a kid in the 70's wanted to play Cowboys and Indians, the moms wouldn't say that it's politically incorrect or racist, they would yell out the front door *"Come home when you hear the 6 'oclock firehouse alarm and wear your coat!"* It was a great time to be alive and we knew better than to shoot each other with anything other than the cap gun. If we didn't have a cap gun, it took about 5 seconds to find a tree branch that resembled a gun. We didn't mean any disrespect to Cowboys or Indians and we knew the difference between shooting each other in this game of tag and shooting someone in real life with a real gun. The whole concept didn't need any further explanation. It was a game and we instinctively knew the difference. Kids aren't dumb. We have managed to brainwash our kids and make them fearful of everything. How have we accomplished this? Lies, Lies and more.... LIES.

Good Gun Bad Guy

Let's take a kid who is 10 years old now and put him in Doc Brown's DeLorean. We'll send him back to 1976 and drop him in the middle of the woods with a bunch of other kids who are in the process of playing Cowboys and Indians. How do think that would play out? Let's have some fun.

Billy: Who are you?

Emerson: My name is Emerson. So... I think I'm lost.

Billy: What's that?

Emerson: Umm, my iPhone....?

Billy: Whatever. You better grab a stick or you're gonna die.

Emerson: What do you mean?

Billy: HURRY UP! Get behind that tree! You'll be on my team.

Emerson: What? What are you talking about?

Billy: The Cowboys, man. Grab a stick now or you're gonna get us both killed.

<Billy pushes Emerson behind the tree and he falls to his knees.>

Emerson: I dropped my phone and my new school clothes are messed up now.

Billy: Shhhhh. Be quiet. Just wait here.

Emerson: I'm not gonna chill in the woods. It's all dirty.

Billy: Chill? It's not even cold out here. What's with the weird shoes?

178

Emerson: Look, I don't know what's going on but I need to get home. I'm not getting any signal.

Billy: I'll go up to the old car and when it's safe, I'll give you the signal. Then you meet me up there but don't get shot! Here, here's your gun.

<Billy breaks a branch of a tree and hands it to Emerson>

Emerson: What do you mean guns? Get shot?!

Billy: Don't worry about it. If you listen to me, you'll be ok. I'm gonna go. Stay here and shut up or they'll shoot you.

<Emerson falls to the ground, face down, and puts both hands over the back of his head with his elbows covering his ears.>

Emerson: How are you getting a signal? Do you have a hotspot?

<Billy dashes from behind the tree and dives chest first into a mud puddle behind an old, rusted out abandoned car.>

Billy: <whispers loudly> C'mon, hurry up!

Emerson: I'm not going anywhere. I'm scared. What's going on?

Billy: If you don't get over here, you're gonna get ambushed. C'mon!

<Emerson slowly crawls toward Billy while looking down at his phone, still trying to get a signal>

Billy: Hurry up! You're in the line of fire! What are you stupid?!

<Three high pitched popping sounds and a voice is heard from off in the distance>

Tommy: You're dead!

179

Good Gun Bad Guy

Billy: Alright, you got us! SAFE!!!

<Tommy keeps shooting his cap gun>

Billy: SAFE! I said SAFE Tommy! Stop shooting!

<Tommy and two other boys emerge from the woods and meet Billy and Emerson at the rusty car>

Tommy: Who's this?

<Emerson slowly peeks his head out from behind the car (dirt has collected in the tears running down his cheeks)>

<Emerson sobs with relief, realizing he is only involved in a game>

Emerson: I'm Emerson. Somehow I got lost and ended up in your game. I really need to get home. I'm not supposed to play guns.

Tommy: We're not "playing guns." We're Cowboys and Indians and if you're on Billy's team, you're an Indian and you're dead.

Emerson: You're not supposed to talk like that.

Tommy: What? <Tommy turns to Billy with a confused look on his face>

Billy: I don't know who this kid is Tommy.

Tommy: Hey, what's that thing?

Emerson: That's my iPhone. What's with you guys? You act like you never saw an iPhone. I've been trying to get a signal. I don't have any bars.

Tommy: Let me see that. <Tommy rips the phone out of Emerson's hand>

Emerson: Hey, give that back!

Tommy: Billy, It's like Spock's Tricoder or something.

Emerson: What are you talking about? You guys don't have phones?

Billy: Sure, we have phones. At home. Duh.

Emerson: Sooo... you guys are gonna get in trouble for using guns and talking about Indians. If your Principal finds out, you might even get suspended.

Billy: Tommy's Dad is the Principal. He bought him that gun.

Tommy: Here, take your stupid Tricoder. <Tommy pushes Emerson's iPhone into his stomach>

Emerson: Ouch! You know, I can have you arrested for that. My Mom says guns are bad and cause school shootings. We should never joke around about them.

This story is made up of course, but it brings to light the way lies can influence children, change their perspective on life and alter the course of future generations. What beliefs will Emerson instill in his children with respect to guns? Somehow in recent decades we have allowed the gun narrative to get high-jacked by liberals and the anti-gun minority. I think it is done with some level of good intent because some of them actually believe that guns *are* the cause of violence. But regardless of their intent, a lie is a lie. The demonizing of guns is a lie that can have deadly results.

You may think that gun deaths have skyrocketed in recent years due to the heightened rhetoric around the topic but the truth is quite the opposite. Here are some facts that the Anti-2nd Radicals don't want you to know.

The FBI "Crime in the United States" report found 8,124 murders committed with firearms in 2014, down from 8,454 in 2013. That represents a 3.9 percent drop year over year and the lowest rate of any year included in the report.

The FBI also reported in their 2012 "Uniform Crime Reports" that total firearm murders were down to 8,855 from 9,528 in 2007

So why has the feeling toward guns changed so much? Because the Anti-2nd Amendment Radicals know that if they craft lies carefully they can convince people and build their army of Anti-Gunners. In a democracy the majority rules. This is why they are working very hard to *be* the majority. They're not there yet but could be soon if we don't take action. The left-wing of the government and the Democratic party in general has done everything they can to convince people to hate and fear guns. They have harnessed the media, the movie industry and the educational system. The focus is on pushing a consistent message that guns are bad to anyone within earshot. This includes our children. How long, at this rate, do you think it will take to create a country full of Emersons?

We already know that Anti-2nd Radicals lie about statistics and present completely false statements as facts. Dana Loesch talks about this in her book "Hands off My Gun." Here are just a couple examples. The Radicals will tell the world that guns cause more deaths than they prevent. The truth is, guns are used to stop crimes more often than they are used to commit crimes. Another beauty is when they say anyone can buy a gun. This is absurd. Anyone can't buy a gun. As a matter of fact it has become increasingly more difficult and the waiting periods can be very lengthy for law-abiding citizens to purchase firearms. My goal is not as much to fill this book with statistics but rather help uncover the reasons why the Anti-2nd Radicals lie. The intent behind the lies is much more important in our fight to defend our rights and move toward a 100% pro-gun America.

Let's take the first one. By continually perpetuating the lie that guns are used to commit more crimes than they prevent, the narrative and overall sentiment changes in their favor. The idea here is to make sure as many people as possible have a fearful feeling in their gut and associate that feeling with guns. This lie presupposes that fewer guns will equal less crime. This is a game of word-association. Here's an example of how misleading this game can be to people who aren't paying attention. What would you say if I asked you to name of the "King of Pop?" Of course you would name Michael Jackson. But the truth is Mariah Carey and the Beatles have more number one hits. "Ok, big deal." Well, Tell that to Mariah Carey. It actually probably doesn't matter that much to Mariah but the point is that with enough emphasis and continuous conditioning, people can be programmed to believe things that are not based in truth. They can also be trained to associate feelings with things. Imagine how many people think guns take more lives than they save. Plenty. But you say *"It doesn't matter. It's not true."* Oh, but it does matter. *It's* what really matters. The narrative is the goose that produces the golden eggs. In other words, the narrative produces beliefs in people, those beliefs dictate the ideology we all must live by.

How about the simple yet powerful lie that anyone can buy a gun? Why do you think the Anti-2nd Radicals use this? What is the implication? Think about it for a minute. *"Anyone can buy guns."* This one is perfect because the word "anyone" helps the unsuspecting armchair warrior envision the worst possible candidates as gun owners. They want you to envision rapists, murderers, gang members, drug addicts and even little kids with guns. It doesn't matter if it is true. All that matters is the visual impression they can tattoo on the brains of voters. As long as Sally Soccer-Mom envisions murderous maniacs walking into a gun shop and leaving with an assortment of really scary black extra-shooty guns, they've achieved their goal. They can be found out later to be liars and to have completely misrepresented the facts but in the grand scheme of things it doesn't matter. Their mission has already been accomplished. Manipulating the internal representation of unsuspecting Americans is all that matters to them. It doesn't matter if it is true! That is why the war of statistics doesn't work. We are constantly pushing factual statistics in their faces and they don't care. How many Anti-2nd Amendment Radicals have converted because they were proved wrong on statistics? Exactly...... Zero! Imagery and visceral reactions are what sway public opinion. It always has and it always will. It's a human nature thing.

In America it would seem the media narrative is usually the opposite of reality. This is especially true with guns and criminals. Guns are used 60 times more often to protect lives than they are to take lives, but you wouldn't know that if you took the media at their word.

The Anti-2nd Amendment Radical group "Moms Demand Action" seems to be a bit truth-challenged too when it comes to...well most everything they spew. Taking credit for anti-gun policies that they had nothing to do with appears to be one of their favorite pastime.

According to President and CEO Preston Atkinson of the 700+ burger franchise "Whataburger," the company has had an informal ban on open-carry in their restaurants for "a long time." You may or may not agree with the policy but that's not the point. The "Moms" have claimed to be the driving force in that decision. They also claim it was a recent development. Well, not true and not true again. First of all Atkinson points out that the decision was made long ago and no specific group had any influence of his choice.

"Whataburger supports customers' Second Amendment rights and we respect your group's position, but we haven't allowed the open carry of firearms in our restaurants for a long time (although we have not prohibited licensed conceal carry). It's a business decision we made a long time ago," Atkinson said.

It sounds to me like Atkinson is implying the "Moms Demand" should stop riding the coattails of anti-gun policy just for the media coverage.

So, why is this important? Well, first of all it's important to show how some less-ethical groups will lie just to get a narrative out to the public. The idea here is for them to change public opinion and build notoriety for their group so they have momentum going into their next misleading venture. By claiming that they were the cause of the so called "gun free" policy at Whataburger, they appear to have the power to influence. The truth is, they don't. As a matter of fact, support at their rallies is dismal at best. If they get caught in a lie however, the message and internal representation in the minds of the people is already out there. They could apologize or retract a wrongful statement if they choose to, but the damage has already been done. And that's all that really matters to them – public perception.

Another important fact to point out with respect to this and other media hoaxes, is that when these claims are made, other media outlets pick up the story and further spread the misleading nonsense. In the wake of the "Moms/Whataburger" sham, Newsweek released a headline that said, "Whataburger to Armed Customers: Keep Your Guns at Home." They also stated, "Advocates for the group (Moms Demand Action) have persuaded managers at other major businesses to change their gun policies, including Starbucks, Chipotle, Sonic Drive-In and Target."

The Newsweek drivel is not true either. As a matter of fact Starbucks Chief Executive Howard Schultz released a letter stating:

"For these reasons, today we are respectfully requesting that customers no longer bring firearms into our stores or outdoor seating areas—even in states where "open carry" is permitted—unless they are authorized law enforcement personnel."

The carefully calibrated statement stopped short of banning guns (as have statements from a handful of other retailers). At Starbucks's more than 11,000 outlets in the U.S. Mr. Schultz said he wants *"to give responsible gun owners the chance to respect our request"* and doesn't want to put employees in the position of confronting armed customers." *"Starbucks doesn't plan to post signs in its stores asserting its position,"* a spokesman said. By not posting signs, businesses are not committing to a strict 'Gun Free" policy, instead they are making a political statement just shy of the responsibility to enforce such a policy. They are trying to appease the Anti-Gunners while trying to avoid being labeled "Anti-Gun."

So, is that a policy or a request? I think it's clear that Schultz specifically made a request to pacify the anti-gun latte drinkers but it doesn't seem like policy, definitely is not law and does not appear to be a result of the loony-toon group of anti-gun Moms. They created all this nonsense to instill fear in Anti-Gunners and create division among good people of the community.

While groups like "Moms Demand Action" and other Anti-2nd Radicals push lies and misleading propaganda it is our responsibility as law-abiding gun owners and honest Americans to hold them accountable and make them answer to their mistruths because the lies they spread permeate society and create legions of ill-informed, fearful anti-gun warriors.

I was talking to my friend Nate. Nate was trying to explain to me how dangerous so-called "assault weapons" are and how they are created for the sole purpose of killing mass amounts of people quickly. He tried convincing me that when you hold down the trigger of an AR-15 semi-automatic rifle the bullets just spray out. Nate then went on to pound his fists on the table in defiance and said there is nothing I could say that would convince him that these weapons should not be completely banned from our society.

This is yet another example of misguided people expressing their delusion out of fear and frustration. When I was finally able to calm Nate down, I began explaining to him that semi-automatic rifles don't spray bullets and the term "assault weapon" is a term created by the anti-gun left for the purpose of stigmatizing guns. I explained to Nate that "AR" stands for ArmaLite rifle, which is the name of a company that developed this style rifle back in the 1950s and not "assault rifle." I also explained that the AR style rifles are designed to look like the M-16 which indeed is a military rifle, but the difference between the two are night and day with respect to the fully-automatic capability of the M-16. The AR-15 is among the most widely purchased rifle for hunting and sporting use. Contrary to Nate's "spraying bullets" myth, they only fire one round with each trigger pull. Unfortunately Nate has been so indoctrinated that it wouldn't seem like there is any hope in bringing him back to reality. He would not accept what I was saying and refused to engage in a thoughtful conversation as soon as I started to present facts. He only engaged when he was able to loudly and angrily express his views. Otherwise, he would change the subject.

I must say it is frustrating to witness such a misguided group of people completely hung-up on lies and myths about guns. The AR is an area where these lies run rampant. The lies and false narrative around these guns is so thick that the faux terminology has even worked its way into the language of Pro-Gunners. When you hear a gun owner refer to an AR-15 as an "assault rifle" you know the propaganda has permeated society in a huge way. This was the plan of Democrats back in the 1990s when they implemented the term "assault rifle" or "assault weapon" into the conversation. You have to give them credit for their creativity and persistence because it worked. They managed to take an ugly term and attach it to Americas favorite sporting rifle while simultaneously scaring the hell out of people.

Once the stigma gained traction in society, the anti-gun politicians jumped on the opportunity to implement as many restrictions as possible using the fear of the people as fuel for their rampant, ridiculous laws. Democratic Senator, Diane Feinstein, during the Senate and House press conference on the "Assault Weapons Ban of 2013" said, *"I continue to believe that drying up the supply of military-style assault weapons is an important piece of the puzzle—and the data backs this up. These weapons were designed for the military and have one purpose: to kill as many people as possible, as quickly as possible. They are the weapon of choice for grievance killers, gang members and juveniles, and they shouldn't be on the streets. Let me be clear, Assault weapons allow criminals to fire more shots, wound and kill more individuals and inflict greater damage. The research supports that. A ban on assault weapons was never meant to stop all gun crimes, it was meant to help stop the most deadly mass shootings. That's why it needs to be a part of the discussion, or rampages like Sandy Hook will continue to happen."*

Feinstein clearly uses a lot of rhetoric and lies such as the idea

188

that these guns are designed to kill as many people as possible. Not true. They are designed to be a rugged low-maintenance sporting rifle. She then followed up with rhetoric about allowing criminals to fire more shots and the weapon of choice for juveniles. Really? How many more shots can they shoot and how many kids have you seen running around with AR-15s? Then she decided to implement the notion that they inflict greater damage. Greater damage than what? Finally, to imply that the Sandy Hook shooting would not have happened had it not been for this type of rifle is absolutely preposterous.

Next, Feinstein outlined the restrictions and specifications of what defines an "assault rifle" and what features she believes you should and shouldn't be allowed to have. This is where the idiocy comes in. The following was taken from Feinstein's website in January 2016 referring to the "Assault Weapons Ban of 2013."

Mass shootings in Newtown, Aurora, and Tucson have demonstrated all too clearly the need to regulate military-style assault weapons and high capacity ammunition magazines. These weapons allow a gunman to fire a large number of rounds quickly and without having to reload.

What the bill does:

The legislation bans the sale, transfer, manufacturing and importation of:

All semiautomatic rifles that can accept a detachable magazine and have at least one military feature: pistol grip; forward grip; folding, telescoping, or detachable stock; grenade launcher or rocket launcher; barrel shroud; or threaded barrel.

189

Good Gun Bad Guy

All semiautomatic pistols that can accept a detachable magazine and have at least one military feature: threaded barrel; second pistol grip; barrel shroud; capacity to accept a detachable magazine at some location outside of the pistol grip; or semiautomatic version of an automatic firearm.

All semiautomatic rifles and handguns that have a fixed magazine with the capacity to accept more than 10 rounds.

All semiautomatic shotguns that have a folding, telescoping, or detachable stock; pistol grip; fixed magazine with the capacity to accept more than 5 rounds; ability to accept a detachable magazine; forward grip; grenade launcher or rocket launcher; or shotgun with a revolving cylinder.

All ammunition feeding devices (magazines, strips, and drums) capable of accepting more than 10 rounds.

157 specifically-named firearms.

I always found it idiotic that someone could actually think that if a rifle has a detachable magazine *and* a pistol grip it would somehow be more deadly. But this is the gun-ignorance we have in America.

The shaming of Pro-Gunners and the lies that have been fed to the public about gun owner's positions by President Obama, Hillary Clinton, Diane Feinstein and others should give insight to their overall agenda with respect to the implementation of gun restrictions. The immediate days following a mass-shooting are always the best time for anti-gun politicians to coerce the public into supporting the government as they push to implement restrictions. The biggest thorn in President Obama's side has been the struggle to eliminate military-style rifles ("assault weapons", as they prefer to call them) and "high capacity magazines." His mission has also included relentless attempts to implement "universal background checks."

The tactics in public have included encouraging anyone watching by congratulating them on showing that progress can be done. This is a great technique because it motivates people and helps them feel like they are doing the right thing. It's why you congratulate your middle-schooler for good grades. President Obama said to the American people in 2013, *"When it comes to protecting our children from gun violence, you've shown that progress is possible; that 40 percent means lives saved."* 40 percent referred to the decrease in Minneapolis gun violence. It also implied that anti-gun activism was what accomplished it.

Another technique used is to lie about what gun-owners want. This one is easy because the way this is done leaves no ability to rebut the claim. These things are typically done in a setting where the President's words are the last and only thing heard. Any denouncement or accusations by the NRA or pro-gun advocates must be done later in the press. Typically by that time, the same people who heard the lies are not around to hear the truth. This is why celebrities find it so troubling when gossip-style newspapers make false accusations. Yes, the paper might issue a retraction, but the damage to the celebrity's credibility has already been done. The original readers rarely see the follow-up article.

Referring to what he calls "common sense reform" President Obama said,

"The majority of gun owners think that's a good idea, so if we've got lobbyists in Washington claiming to speak for gun owners, saying something different, we need to go to the source and reach out to people directly. We can't allow those filters to get in the way of common sense."

191

If you look at this statement you will see that it is loaded with rhetoric and misleading accusation. The first and last parts of the statement are worth noting. *"The majority of gun owners think that's a good idea."* First of all, the majority of gun owners do not believe universal background checks are a good idea. That is just a lie. The truth is, law-abiding gun owners do not want the government involved in every single gun transaction. Besides, Obama's "universal background checks" would come with a bunch of other goodies designed to restrict the rights of the Good Guys. UBCs as the President defines them would intrude on simple, private sales and trades amongst family members. You couldn't pass down your pistol or shotgun to your daughter without paying a gun shop to be an intermediary in the transaction. Your pal who no longer hunts, needs a little cash or whose eyes aren't what they used to be can't sell you his shotgun unless you, again, go through an FFL (gun shop/Federal Firearms Licensee) and get approval from Big Brother for your economic transactions by consenting adults. *"Do I have to go through the Federal Library Commission to leave my kids my book collection? The First Amendment gets every benefit of every doubt ...why not the Second?"* The last part of President Obama's statement also includes the implication that Pro-Gunners have no sense. *"We can't allow those filters to get in the way of common sense."*

The shaming of pro-gun advocates was also included in the President's statement when he said,

"If we've got lobbyists in Washington claiming to speak for gun owners, saying something different, we need to go to the source and reach out to people directly."

This was a way of implying that "gun lobbyists" or pro-gun advocate groups such as the NRA are misleading gun owners or lying on behalf of gun owners. This statement is despicable because it

192

attempts to divide gun owners on the topic and implies that in order for the "people" to get the truth, the organizations that represent Pro-Gunners need to be cut out of the conversation because they are a bunch of liars. President Obama and others have used this subtle, unethical technique many times. If you didn't catch that, it's worth a re-read.

Bringing to light the subtle techniques used in the fight to destroy the 2nd Amendment and disarm Americans is important because most often Non-Gunners never catch it yet integrate the misleading rhetoric and lies into their thought process and beliefs. This further indoctrinates them into siding with the Anti-2nd Radicals and supporting laws that are unconstitutional.

The techniques used to accomplish the goals of the anti-gun left are very strategic and effective. They are strategic because the level of damage and influence they have goes unseen in the short-term. In other words, it's very difficult to put your finger on the strategy and they make sure that a strong rebuttal to any accusation is close at hand should you become wise to them. The reason they are so effective is because like a good marketing campaign, the statements and implications are designed to influence you without you knowing it.

The statement from President Obama I used in this example is one of many used to manipulate the thought process of people. It includes the following techniques:

• Congratulate – help the viewer feel good about their involvement in the fight.

• Lie – implement a false base narrative to embolden the scenario they want you to focus on.

- Shame – make the other side look so bad, you would never want to be part of it.

- Divide – reduce the power and ability of their opposition by creating conflict within the targeted group.

If you were the average non-gun owner watching this, which side of the argument would you take?

Here is another statement by President Obama with respect to lies, division and shaming.

"Tell them there's no legislation to eliminate all guns. There's no legislation being proposed to subvert the 2nd Amendment. Tell them specifically what we're talking about. Things that the majority of Americans, when they're asked, support and tell them, now is the time for action. That we're not going to wait until the next Newtown or the next Aurora."

Is it really about the pistol grip? Will the elimination of pistol grips save lives? Of course not. The war on military style rifles is a segue to bigger and better bans. Obviously the intent is to ban these rifles. Then what? Well that's it. Then the Antis will be satisfied and go away, right? Don't bet your lunch on it. Next will be ammo, handguns, and the implementation of more Gun Free Zones.

We tend to accept small violations to our privacy and freedom. We do it with automobile tracking systems, spending & online habit monitoring, mandatory vaccinations, restricted water usage, traffic-light cameras and even regulated light bulbs. *"Oh, it's just a small inconvenience. We'll get used to it."* It's the big violations that we won't tolerate, right? Would you allow the government to chip your children? I know, you're screaming at me for even suggesting it.

"Absolutely not! I would never allow such a thing!" Now ask yourself if you think your great-grandchildren will allow the government to chip their kids. If you had to stop and consider it as a possibility, you are seeing how the progressive implementation of government control is possible. It creeps in. Remember, chipping has already become acceptable. It's even popular to chip our pets. You may have even done it yourself.

When it comes to the 2nd Amendment, if we accept small restrictions and regulations that do nothing to reduce the loss of life, we are allowing the eventual destruction of our right to bear arms. The truth is, many gun restrictions increase the risks to innocent people; Gun Free Zones for instance. The only reason the restrictions are not so painful is because we allow them in small increments. I say *allow them* because we need to take full responsibility for what happens. That's one very distinctive characteristic of Conservatives. Conservatives take responsibility. It's something progressive leaders hate. They would much rather we just submit and join the ranks of their warriors. It would make everything much easier for them.

Although the Anti-2nd Amendment Radicals would like things to move along quicker, they have all the time in the world. They can wait. If we allow the constant implementation of restrictions to continue, our grandchildren will look back in history and say, *"I heard there was a time when people were actually allowed to own guns."* Don't think for a minute that the Diane Feinsteins, Hillary Clintons, Michael Bloombergs and Barack Obamas are stupid because they know nothing about guns. They know they want control and they know how to get it. They just wish it could happen faster. Our saving grace has been the Bill of Rights. Americans were thinking back in 1789. It's a miracle they thought with such clarity and could see this far into the future. They knew how corrupt we could be so they included provisions to help us defend against a destructive, controlling government should it grow so big and try to eat its own.

It would seem that our politicians are either completely oblivious to the real sources of guns involved in crime or they are just trying to keep it from the American people. If they were to expose the illegal underground world of gun sales they would have to focus on something that would not produce instant results and lavish praise from voters. Their lies and misrepresentation about guns when it comes to school shootings is a perfect example of how they embolden the idea that every suburban kid has access to military weaponry and more laws should be implemented to prevent it.

Meanwhile, the illegal gun-runners run rampant. These sales are comprised of but not limited to a combination of stolen guns and straw purchasers who legally buy guns for the purpose of selling on the streets. You would think that the price mark-up on the street would be ten times retail but the truth is, there is so much competition out there in the illegal gun-sale market that often these guns only sell for a couple hundred dollars over retail.

Where is the focus? I don't have to tell you because you see it in the news. The focus is on middle America, Why? Because it is easy to attack the legal gun owner and implement more restrictions. It doesn't do anything to solve the problem; but why solve the problem if you are a politician and can show your constituents that you are doing what they want?

So while President Obama and Hillary Clinton can shed a tear for the cameras, raise their voices, pound their fists in anger and promise the public that they will do whatever it takes to stop the violence (if you'll just vote for them), they fail to reveal the fact that they are really not doing anything productive. Their goal is to show their anti-gun voters that they are fixing the problem of "gun violence" by filling the media with anti-gun rhetoric and lies while the real problem continues to grow. Should any politician truly want to fix the problem of crimes committed with guns, they would go to the streets and show the people what they are doing to break up the illegal trafficking activity among the drug dealers and criminals. The truth is, the number of laws implemented that deter criminals is exactly zero but what the heck, it gets votes.

So while we have the smokescreen of school-shootings fueled by rhetoric and lies designed to put the focus on guns, our elected officials spend no time on exposing the destructive, angry, ideological behavior and mental derangement of the human beings committing the crimes. What's the real problem? It lies within us. But the truth is, putting the focus on fixing humanity is not on the list of ways to acquire quick results and voter acceptance, so they continue to lie.

Good Gun Bad Guy

9. I'M RIGHT, YOU'RE WRONG

After listening to an anti-gunner go on and on about how only cops should have guns, I asked him; "If someone were to break into your house and threaten the lives of your family with a gun, do you have a cop to defend and protect them?"

He got pissed off, grabbed his latte and stormed out.

The amazing thing about Anti-Gunners and Anti-2nd Radicals is that those same people will buy auto insurance and homeowners insurance yet choose not to insure their own safety. The idea that someone would buy insurance for their car but none for their life may not make sense to you until you begin to understand the psychological hold that has been placed on them. I'm not talking about the life-insurance you purchase that offers a cash reward to your surviving family members after you die, I'm talking about the life insurance that preserves your life so you don't die. The problem is not necessarily that *they* choose to be unarmed and helpless. The problem is they try to make you and me unarmed and helpless right along with them.

Not only do Anti-Gunners choose unarmed and helpless as a way of life, they have developed a number of arguments to justify it and they work hard to convince others that it is a good condition to be in. This is irresponsible in a society like ours. In America we have people living among us that want to do us harm and have the means to do it. We don't always know who they are. Not only are you at risk when you choose the condition of unarmed and helpless but you also affect everyone around you--family, friends, co-workers and even people you may not even know.

As much as people may like to believe they are independent, the truth is, we live in an interdependent society and we all affect each other. We also have a responsibility to protect each other. When an element of our society fights to make us unsafe by pursuing personal disarmament because they believe it is a good idea, they become a danger to our society. The 2nd Amendment is the most important amendment in our Bill of Rights because it's the only one that actually talks about the right to defend our lives from the destructive ideas of this dangerous group of people. That is why there is such a fierce battle to preserve it.

The clash of ideologies we see in America is astounding. How is it that we as human beings can be so divided on issues? Take a look at guns, abortions, capitalism, welfare, war, immigration or any other hot topic. You will find American's opinions split down the middle. People are not only split but take a very strong stance in support of their view and seem to have no tolerance for the other.

It also seems that in most cases if you side with a group (Conservative or Liberal) on one topic, you tend to agree on all. If there are one or two topics you stray from your group on, it is usually a topic you don't talk about. Could it be that our brains are designed to think one way or the other, or could it be something else that is causing us to take sides? I do believe the split is politically driven, but in a way that utilizes the internal weaknesses we have as humans. I believe we are driven by our need to be "right."

This topic became very interesting after I witnessed a conversation about abortion. The woman who was "for abortion" got so irate that she was belittling the woman who was against it. The woman who was against abortion believed that it was wrong to do. Their definition of *wrong* was obviously different, and that distinction could have been part of the problem. But the real interesting (and scary) part was the fact that the woman supporting abortion could be so destructive and demeaning in supporting her view. It literally came down to name calling and personal insults.

This got me thinking,

- *"What would it mean to some people if they were to admit their views or beliefs were inconsistent or without merit?"*
- *"What if they were able to see the other person's point of view?"*
- *"What would it mean about them as a person?"*
- *"What would it mean about someone if they were wrong?"*

Being "wrong" to some is a matter of simple awareness and recalibration. Ask a CEO how often he or she is wrong and you'll most likely find out that the answer is more often than not. This is because some people use failure as a tool to grow. I remember creating a business plan for a new company launch and my advisors watched every keystroke and calculation like a hawk. I was held accountable to every financial projection and every piece of market information I presented. If something didn't make sense, seemed unfounded or wasn't backed up with sound data, I was questioned. During the process I was often wrong. I learned early on that I was not going to get away with passing anything off as fact because I was scrutinized every step of the way. Every data point I presented needed to be backed up by more data because it would be used to build the company model. If the initial data had weak merit it would affect what was to come after. You wouldn't build a house on an inferior foundation. Therefore I was held accountable and it didn't feel good. It didn't feel good because being held accountable shined a spotlight on me being unprepared. I was caught in the act. It was embarrassing and I quickly learned that if I wanted to build this model and ultimately turn it into a working company, I needed to put in the time necessary and pay attention to every single piece of data.

The pain of being "found out" for some people is more than they can bear because they take it to mean something about them as a person. When someone is exposed as lying or misrepresenting the data, they get a feeling of embarrassment. Embarrassment is nothing more than exposure but can be devastating to some who may not have strong self-esteem. This is why Anti-Gunners stick to their narrative amidst strong opposition and conflicting data. They can't be wrong because it would mean they have been dishonest or even worse, incorrect. Anti-Gunners already live with a terrifying fear so any admission of guilt or data-slanting would be devastating to them. How do you deal with someone who cannot be "wrong?" Well, you don't throw more data in their face. Remember, they have data, plenty of it and if it doesn't serve their objective they will get some that does. They hope you go on a scavenger hunt to prove their data wrong because when you do they will change the topic again. The data battle is endless. We need to understand what is going on in their minds to better deal with the dishonesty and bias.

As humans, we are insecure in many ways. We need reassurance often. For example, let's say you just bought a boat-load of stock in a company called Wizbang and the day after you bought it the news announced that they made a merger with another company causing the stock to almost double. You'd feel pretty secure about your

202

position. But let's say as soon as you bought your Wizbang stock everyone you know told you that the company will tank and you made a horrible decision. You'd probably feel insecure or at least question your decision. The feeling of insecurity can apply to a wide range of things; from not knowing why your car is making a grinding noise, to going into public with a bad haircut. The truth is, we feel better about ourselves when more people agree with us.

- What does it mean about me (as a person) if others disagree with me?
- Why does it matter what other people think of me?
- Why do we care if people agree with our views?

Most people (if they're being honest) will come up with answers that point to validation or something similar. *"The more people that agree with me, the more valid my argument is."* At least that's what we think. This is so important to some people that they will argue their point to the extent that it turns into personal bashing, name calling, ridiculing and sometimes even physical confrontation. That's how important it is to some people to be "right" about something.

So what causes this need to be right and why is it that some people don't care who agrees with them? It could come down to confidence, self-esteem or the need to feel like the victim. Those who are confident don't need validation from anyone and have no need to rally people to their side of the argument. Those who are unsure of themselves or have doubts about the validity of their cause will argue to the death because one more person on their side validates their claim a little bit more and helps them feel more secure in their own beliefs. Often people may have doubts about their own beliefs. Many times a person's beliefs can define them. You may know someone who supports a cause or is an avid sports fan to the point that the activity is synonymous with them. In other words,

203

when you see them they somehow project that thing. Conversation always comes around to that thing and there is no doubt that they support the cause. What would it mean about that person if their cause was proven to be invalid, their mission ended or their team loses? To some, it's a shot to their ego, some are lost because they no longer have the thing they devoted a large portion of their time to and some are devastated because they focused their entire existence around that cause or activity; It became a huge part of who they are. Anti-gun activism is that thing to some people.

When a person is all alone on a topic, they may stop and wonder why. Some will fear the thought because they think the rest of the world might know something they don't and some might wonder why everyone else hasn't seen reality yet. Again, this comes from the level of attachment and/or the level of understanding the person has with respect to the topic. Standing alone with your beliefs amidst contradiction and even confrontation is a great measure of confidence and strength in your personal ethics and beliefs.....or is it ignorance, stubbornness and delusion?

There is a level of perceived righteousness ingrained in the victim mentality that fuels people to further blame others. This victim mindset feels good to some people. It feels comfortable thinking that the difficult choices are someone else's to make or the bad things that happen in the world are someone else's fault. For some, it feels comfortable and safe within the bubble of honorable-virtue, even if it is fake. Being able to blame someone or something else creates the fantasy that the "blamer" is the "Good Guy." Let's face it, sometimes owning up to our own actions and mistakes can be a painful reality check. Sometimes having to own our failures helps us see where we were wrong and how we can change. In many cases Anti-Gunners use the illusion of self-righteousness to justify their argument against guns and never admit they may be wrong in their views. The more they operate in this mental environment, the more indignant they become. This causes them to feel even more justified in punishing others for having an interest in guns and gives them license to blame responsible gun owners for irresponsible policies they themselves support. In other words, by pointing a finger and saying, "There it is. That's the problem," it takes the focus off the "blamer." Yes, even in their own mind, they justify their accusations and build a sense of righteousness. To admit they have been delusional or just plain wrong becomes impossible for them at a certain point. This is why it sometimes feels like talking to a brick wall when trying to explain pro-gun ideals to an Anti-Gunner. They can't allow themselves to admit to any of it or they would risk their own dignity.

If you notice when some Anti-Gunners talk about guns they do it with a destructive tone and use every bit of language they can to cast the gun in the most heinous light. They'll say things like *"The security guard had his gun in plain sight. I could have easily grabbed it and started killing people."* A statement like that is a good indication of what is going on in the mind of the person. The reason they say things like that is because they are fearful and can only envision guns killing people. They've been programmed to only see death and destruction when the idea of a gun enters their mind. The really disturbing thing is the idea that they also envision *themselves* taking the gun and killing people just because it's there. It is almost as if they believe the gun would posses them to commit the violent act. Understanding this much about Anti-Gunners helps us see why they are so adamant about eliminating guns from society. They may not trust anyone else with guns because they wouldn't trust themselves with guns.

It works like this. When someone accuses you of something, it's often because they have been guilty of the exact same thing. You've heard the stories of the jealous husband or wife convinced that their spouse was cheating, only to be unveiled that their jealousy was created out of their own guilt because they in fact were the one being unfaithful all along. Anytime someone thinks they know what you're thinking, it's because they've thought those exact same thoughts. You can't imagine what someone is thinking unless you have had the same thoughts in your own mind. You can't imagine how someone feels unless you have experienced the feeling yourself.

Some people may be convinced that they know how you "feel" by the expression on your face. Has anyone ever accused you of being angry when you were not? *"Well you looked like you were mad,"* they'd say. This is called "projection." It's a concept that was coined by Sigmund Freud in 1841. It was a term that was defined to shed light on how and why people blame others and how the thought process is developed and constructed in the mind of the accuser. The accusations or assumption of how someone else "feels" or what they are thinking is developed through data in the accusers mind. We can only imagine thoughts or feelings that we ourselves have personally experienced. So when someone says, *"I could have easily grabbed the gun and started killing people,"* they had to envision themselves grabbing the gun and killing people prior to saying it.

There is an argument for gun restrictions that is used quite frequently by a group of ideologically-challenged gun-grabbers that says "we" can't be trusted with guns. I guess "we" means Americans in general. This is the "Wild West" imagery they like to depict. The notion is that we must further restrict gun ownership because some people, if in possession of a gun, would flip out and kill people if their fast food order is wrong or someone cuts them off in traffic. The idea that people will die in public for the most trivial of reasons is a belief that runs through a good portion of our society. We know it is fear-based, childish and without any sense of logic but it's dangerous to give these people a seat at the negotiating table. Although I agree that some people should not have guns, the argument they use is based in the premise that the average person, under the right stressful situation and because they have a gun would lose it and go insane. In other words, many actually believe that the gun causes people to become killers.

The facts show that legally licensed gun owners never seem to prove this theory correct. As a matter of fact, it's the exact opposite. Yes, sometimes the guns used in crimes are legally owned, but very rarely by the shooter himself. Many are stolen. I have to wonder why it is that Anti-2nd Radicals envision the gun making the person commit murder. If you ask a gun owner if they thought a person could be influenced by a gun they would think you're crazy. The answer would be "of course not." But somehow Antis still try to push the idea that people would be influenced and lose all sense of free will as soon as they have a gun in their hands. Maybe they doubt *themselves* and assume that all people are just as free-will-challenged as they are. It almost makes you question the trustworthiness of a person who has those thoughts in their mind and those doubts about the ability of people to make their own decisions.

In this hypothetical scenario, an otherwise normal person gets completely deranged because of the gun. In other words, the gun made him do it. Had he not possessed the gun, he would have quietly taken his burger (with pickles) and accepted it. But because he had a gun on him, he shot up the joint. I know, I know, it sounds ridiculous but the thought process is what we are talking about. Among the Anti-Gunners I have interviewed, some believe this is something that could happen.

My goal here is not to rationalize whether or not this type of gun-reactive behavior is likely, but to expose the thought process of the Anti-Gunners that actually think these thoughts on a daily basis.

207

It's not so unbelievable that someone would flip out and kill people over pickles on their burger, but that some people would think it could be caused by the mere presence of a gun, is a much scarier thought to me. Here's why. In order for someone to believe that people are that emotionally reactive and can be moved to kill others for such a trivial thing like an incorrect food order, the person concocting the notion must have those thoughts in their own mind. I would question the emotional-reactivity of a person harboring that thought. Yes, them, for thinking that way. This is actually a thought that many Anti-Gunners will use in support of their gun-control agenda. They don't understand that the destructive murderous thought process is in *their* own mind. The problem on the pro-gun side is that Pro-Gunners don't recognize this and rather than holding the Antis accountable, Pro-Gunners end up defend themselves against the ridiculous accusation. Why in the world would we responsible gun owners want to entertain a debate with someone who comes from this reactive, fear based position?

Another example of thought projection is when someone feels guilty for stealing so they accuse you of stealing. You can't imagine what someone else is thinking unless you yourself can process those same thoughts. Otherwise it would be unfathomable to you. In other words, incapable of being understood. So to think people would go crazy just because they have a gun in their possession says everything about the person concocting the idea.

The idea that people would try to ban guns because they don't trust *themselves* around them is a disturbing thought. We can do something about this. We can help people understand more about guns. We can educate them on how guns works, the proper use of guns and how to safely handle and control them. We can teach them how guns save lives and how important they are to maintain a civilized society. What Anti-2nd Amendment Radicals are trying to do is take guns out of existence because they have a horrific fear of
208

them. Rather than confront their own internal struggles and beliefs, they would much rather see guns just go away.

My suggestion to the gun grabbers is to go into the inner-cities and high crime areas where gun laws are the strictest and take the illegally possessed guns out of the hands of the criminals and gang members. They should demand that those guns be turned over immediately. That would never happen, but implementing laws and restrictions on the Good Guys is much safer for them because law-abiding citizens comply. The hypocrisy from the liberal-left is glaringly apparent. It's why you will never see groups like "Moms Demand Action" or "Everytown for Gun Safety" protesting on the south side of Chicago. They would much rather rally on Main St. in Knoxville, TN. I guess Chicago is too dangerous for them. Wouldn't it make sense that these groups put their money where their mouth is and go to the areas where the most gun crimes are being committed?

Good Gun Bad Guy

10. BUILDING UTOPIA

This Utopian dreamland may take awhile. In the meantime, I'll carry.

Utopia is an imagined society where everything is perfect. There is no crime, everyone is kind to each other, people are always safe, people don't say things that might hurt the feelings of others, everyone has the same amount of money, people are polite and there are no Bad Guys.

Sounds great huh? Yes there are actually people who believe, that with strong regulations, and endless laws and restrictions, this type of society can be achieved. The movie Demolition Man always comes to mind when I think about Utopia. In the movie, all the "bad" people were forced to live underground while the "good" people enjoyed the perfect life. Yes there were cops to keep order but everyone complied. If you said a word that was not allowed, you would get a citation. The government monitored the public's every move and every word. Sounds like Political Correctness.

Journal entry from the future 2062

I woke up to the sound of Taylor Swift on the Transnet. I just love the oldies. That music reminds me of when I was five years old and Mom & Dad would take me to the mall. We would drive in an old car called a leaf. I remember the car well because my Dad would talk about all the gas he was saving by driving it. Funny how my parents had to manually control their own vehicle.

As I made my way to the kitchen for my daily injections and audio download, the local halo-gram report announced that they made an arrest right in my city quad district. Apparently they found the Ze who has been using the "F" word in public domain. So happy! We just cannot have that type of violent behavior.

My new outdoor fiber suit has been detoxed and is waiting for me. Great news! Government Hill has added a colorful stripe to this month's design. I always feel special when my district is first to present the new fashion. I almost got written up last week because my cuff was folded back. It's not fair to everyone else that I stand out. Luckily I was able to prove that the mishap was caused by a defect in the material.

On my way to the Cube I passed an old friend traveling in the opposite direction on the Triple-Rail. We smiled at each other. I was careful not to let anyone else see, as I wouldn't want to be accused of sexual misconduct. Especially today because it's my birthday and I plan on treating myself to a flavor bar tonight. It's not often that we are allowed to experience food with taste so I don't want to lose the opportunity. It's another one of the few pleasures I remember as a child. Thirty-two years ago today in 2030 I came into this World. If you told me how much things would change, I would have never believed you. Not that you would lie of course because I would never accuse someone of that.

It was a pretty uneventful day at Cube. My supervisor said I completed my work with excellence. Ze then congratulated everyone else for my achievement. It wouldn't be fair if I was the only one to receive such a high honor, but I know I earned it even if I'm not allowed to take full credit. My best friend Tanz was feeling disrespected because someone raised their voice when the Sky Cam glitched. I told Ze to go to "Safe Zone" and wait ten minutes. It happens from time to time and there is never a good reason for it but with a half hour counsel session the victims of public aggression usually feel safe again. Thankfully we have a society where death-crimes are non-existent. We have had virtually no death-crime since 2035. That's when mandatory chipping went into effect. All citizen-property of Chinerica were chipped. What a great advancement our society has made. Now, anytime someone commits a wrong-doing, their chip is accessed by Government Hill and their prefrontal cortex is shut down.

When I got home from Cube, I said hi to Boko, my dog. Well, virtual dog. Real animals are not allowed due to disease and the potential danger they can cause to others. Virtual pets are wonderful because they are intelligent and very playful.

Tomorrow I will go to the Old American Museum. I enjoy going there because I get a sense of what it was like to live in a barbaric time. People had guns, they drove vehicles and they even consumed mind-altering substances. It must have been mayhem. There were privately owned businesses and people even exchanged currency. I wonder if the people who had more money than others felt guilty. It is so unfair for someone to have more than others. Government Hill regulates all belongings and entertainment so no one has more than others. I remember hearing stories from my parents about how they could go wherever they wanted to go completely undetected by government and the citizens were able to vote for the leaders that would run the country. How did they think that people were responsible enough to pick who would be in charge? It must have been scary to have that kind of freedom and responsibility. There where riots in the streets and before the Chinese Republic took over, the people of America had the freedom to speak any words they wanted to. There wasn't even a restricted word list. I can understand how that

213

would be a terrible thing. It was like you could say whatever you wanted to say completely unlimited. That's just not fair to people who are emotionally reactive to certain words.

At the museum, you can see the guns that people used to be allowed to own. They shot bullets so powerful they could go right through your body and you would die. I couldn't imagine living in a time when people would be just running around shooting at each other all the time for no reason but the history files don't lie. If it wasn't for the Bank of China buying all the American banks and taking all their assets we could still be living in an unregulated, dangerous society where people are able to do whatever they want. I heard stories about the year 2025 when the Chinese banks bought out the American banks and called all the mortgages. American families were forced to leave their homes and Chinese families moved in.

I still have memories of my parents before I turned 18, even though I spent countless days in the reprogramming chamber after they were degenerated. I understand why government limits life-years but occasionally memories will still surface and I feel a moment of sadness. I understand however that if we were all allowed to live to natural end, there would be far too many people in population. It's only fair to regulate the number of years we are allowed to live.

Is this future a possibility? If it were to become a reality, a few things would have to be coordinated. The most important of which would be for people to comply. The way to make people comply is to use leverage. Leverage can be found in emotional control, physical control and financial control.

Emotional control could be gained by creating fear in the minds of the people then providing a way to reduce that fear. If people are scared enough they will gravitate toward the entity that promises them safety.

Physical control can be achieved by simply overpowering people. Disarming them and creating strategies to reduce their ability to govern their own lives are ways to break down the human spirit and ambition. Upon realizing that they can't possibly win the fight, they either conform or die in the battle. If power is taken away from people slowly, they may never even recognize it until it's too late.

Financial control could be achieved by making people dependent on government. This could be done in a number of ways. Taking away the ability of people to trade freely, getting them addicted to free hand-outs and helping them develop a sense of entitlement and addiction to things they haven't earned would cause them to give up trying and gravitate toward the hand that feeds them.

Is this future likely?

Is this future the best thing for humanity?

Would you be considered a conspiracy theorist for even considering such a thing?

Of course this story from the future is purely hypothetical and a totally made up fantasy, but is it possible? Are there any signs currently that would indicate us moving in that direction?

In order to create a gun-free society, we must first believe that it's possible to remove all the guns. There are 8.9 guns for every 10 people in America and illegal guns pour in on a daily basis. The 8.9 per 10 people are the ones we know about. There is no conceivable way that guns will ever be removed from our society and if there was, keeping more guns from entering would be even harder. The only people that are restricted are the law-abiding. Ted Nugent made a profound point on gun-grabber Piers Morgan's show with respect to this topic.

Piers Morgan: "If there aren't any guns, nobody gets shot."

Ted Nugent: "And if there isn't any water, no one will drown. Tell you what, you work on the guns and stop the gun violence, I'll work on the water so no one drowns anymore. I'll see you at noon. It's impossible!"

The idea that the Anti-2nd Amendment Radicals think they can get rid of guns is preposterous. The premise that they want to save lives is questionable. They must first ignore the facts to be able to pursue their efforts.

Once we take away the basic premise that removing all the guns is possible, the entire gun free society campaign falls apart. The "gun free society" is based on a premise that is impossible to achieve. In the process of chasing this impossible dream we would be putting millions of good people at risk. Any disarming or restrictions takes a fully capable human being and renders them ineffective against opposition. It's like de-clawing a cat and sending it out into the wild. Wouldn't it make sense that this would be obvious to those in support of a gun free society? If it were obvious to be true, why would they pursue this type of plan and create false data to back it up? Maybe they know that it is an impossible feat but they pursue it anyway. Why would they do that?

The idea of Utopia is sold to the minions through fear manipulation, the need for political correctness, and righteous indignation. It is not done because progressive leaders want Utopia.
216

Utopia is used purely for its attractiveness. The so-called progressive Democratic party wants control. A false Utopia is created only to rally their fighters.

So why in the world would anyone support this kind of regulation against something so vital to our existence?

There is an element of our society that wants Utopia and they believe it can be achieved. You know, a world where everyone is kind to one and other, there is no poverty, everyone has the same amount of money, all are considered equal, everyone is singing Kumbaya in unison and there are no Bad Guys. There is a delusional mindset among us that believes this could actually be possible. It's a fringe element of our society that is becoming more mainstream as the decades go by. In the process of creating this Utopian society many actions would need to be taken. The disarming of citizens is only one of them. You see, if this government-controlled society were to exist, it could not have any opposition. It sounds great in theory, but in the inevitably impossible attempt to create this dreamland we will simultaneously be putting ourselves in grave danger.

You decide how important government is to you. You decide what values you hold as an American and you decide what you are willing to do to preserve the way of life that you want your kids and grandkids to live. I understand that although I like fantasy stories, I also realize that trying to live in a fantasy world is impractical. It may be possible that sometime in the future of humanity a productive moral ethic becomes the dominant way of life, but currently we are just not seeing it. Fooling ourselves into thinking laws, rules and restrictions will change the moral standards of people is an example of people trying to take a fairy-tale and pretend it's reality. I denounce the whole idea that Utopia is an option. I not only denounce it because it doesn't make any logical sense but because it is a childish notion. The pursuit of Utopia is selfish and dangerous.

11. THE TRUTH ABOUT GUNS

"I staunchly oppose guns."

"What about them do you oppose; the use of them by criminals or the use of them by good people defending themselves *against* criminals?"

There is a thought process invoked when you see someone other than a police officer with a handgun on their belt. It's different for everyone. Some might see it as threatening and some might see it as a sign of American liberty being exercised. Some might see it as dangerous and some might see it as just plain smart. The idea that many Anti-Gunners hold onto is that if people are allowed to carry in public, there is a higher likelihood that, otherwise responsible people, will flip out and start shooting others if they are in a bad mood. I can't imagine they actually believe this, but this is the narrative they like to spread. The facts do not show that to be true. As a matter of fact the correlation between the number of guns and the number of crimes is quite the contrary.

As I write this in the beginning of 2016 there are 45 States that allow some form of open-carry. Florida is in the process of becoming the 46th. Should the law be passed in Florida; that would leave California, Illinois, New York, and South Carolina as the only States to restrict open-carry. The debate rolls on among Pro-Gunners and Anti-Gunners as to whether or not open-carry is a good idea. Some will argue that if a terrorist or gang of thugs were in the process of committing a crime, they would take out the person with the gun first because they would be the most likely to foil the plan. Possible. Others may think that if the Bad Guys saw someone with a gun, they would be less inclined to commit the crime. This too is possible.

The truth is, the majority of criminals do not want to get hurt or killed while committing a crime. Criminal interviews have been conducted and have revealed that Bad Guys are far less likely to attack if they have reason to believe their victim is armed. Contrary to popular belief, they are less inclined to commit home robberies at night because armed homeowners are more likely to be home at night. That's when more criminals end up dead. Criminal tactics can be likened to a job of sorts. They tend to do their due diligence when it comes to staking out properties and victims. Their goal is to commit the crime without sustaining injury or death. Many home burglaries are committed in the light of day when homeowners are out of the house.

This brings us to the question of whether or not open-carry is better than concealed-carry. Some contend that it depends on the attacker. If the attacker wants to live to violate another day, they may be less likely to attack you if they saw a .45 on your belt. On the other hand, if the attacker expects and/or wants to die in the process, they may not be deterred and the Good Guy with the gun would probably be their first target.

Some believe that concealed-carry presents the gun owner as a soft target when they really are not. The idea here is that concealing the gun leaves them more vulnerable to attacks. The argument is why not let the Bad Guys know you are armed and can defend yourself? That way they will pass you by and look for their next victim. Open-carry was the norm in the 1800's and concealed carry was considered the behavior of criminals. It would eventually flip to concealed-carry being the most common and open-carry being less common. Is this for the safety of everyone involved or is it for the sole purpose of protecting the fragile emotions of a small group of fearful Anti-Gunners? Whatever the reason, it looks like everyone will have to start getting used to it as gun sales go through the roof and our society's embrace of the gun-culture increases.

In addition to the conceal vs. open-carry debate we still have the question, *"Am I more likely to sustain an injury by using a firearm to resist a physical confrontation or by remaining passive and letting the bad guy violate me?"*

Studies show that it is different for men as opposed to women. The National Crime Victimization Survey conducted by the Department of Justice released some interesting data. Women have a 2.5 times greater chance of sustaining serious injury when offering no resistance to a violent criminal as opposed to using a firearm for self-defense. However, men have only a 1.4 times greater chance of sustaining injuries for playing a passive role. That means taking an active role and protecting oneself pays off on average twice as much.

In an effort to further use his "pen and phone" (President Obama's nice way of saying "executive order" or making decisions without Congress), President Obama once again defied Congress when he directed the Centers for Disease control via executive order to do a study. The study was to research "the causes and prevention of gun violence" and was intended to shut down 2nd Amendment supporters. The study was designed to show an increase in crimes committed with guns, but it failed. In fact, it proved that although gun ownership increased by approximately 1/3, gun crime went down. Is it any wonder why the media didn't shout the findings of the CDC's report from the rooftop?

The idea that gun ownership is on the decline is a narrative that Anti-2nd Radicals would like everyone to believe. The media will push the idea, that with consistent effort & constant demonizing, the elimination or debilitating restriction of private gun ownership is possible. The truth is the exact opposite. Although we are constantly fighting off infringing rules and regulations, the reality is that gun ownership in America is increasing by leaps and bounds. In 2011 the number of American concealed-carry permit holders was approximately 8 million. This information was confirmed in a report by the U.S. Government Accountability Office. As of 2014, that number increased to 11,113,013 equating to 4.8 percent of the population having a concealed-carry license. From 2011 to 2014 the number of new permits grew to 1,390,000 per year. The projected math would indicate that we could expect approximately 16,660,000 or more concealed-carry handgun permits in 2016, equating to 5.2% of the population. What does that mean in the real world? 1 out of every 20 people in the grocery store, coffee shop and local Applebee's are licensed to carry.

The interesting thing about the growth in the number of concealed-carry permit holders is the way it jumped expeditiously during the Obama administration. From 1999-2007 the number of permit holders grew at an average rate of 237,500 per year. During the Obama administration the number of new permit holders averaged 850,000 per year. Coincidence? I think not. Ironic? Yes. Why? Because the rhetoric coming from the Obama administration was a constant stream of gun and gun-owner bashing, yet produced and continues to produce an increase in gun purchases by good American people.

The Obama Presidency was a huge asset to the gun industry. The FBI reported that on Black Friday in 2015 it had processed the most background checks for gun purchases ever recorded in one single day; this, just after the November 13th Paris attacks and more gun restriction rhetoric and threats from President Obama. The number of background checks peaked at an unprecedented 185,345. The total number of background checks for the month of November, 2015 hit 2,243,030; one of the highest months on record. Then, shortly after the December 3rd San Bernardino attack by radical Islamic terrorist Syed Farook and his wife Tashfeen Malik, gun sales surged again. It's ironic how a President who does the most to decrease gun ownership, achieves a skyrocketing increase in sales. Despite his lecturing and rhetoric on how less guns would be safer, he can't quite get the people to fall in step. Maybe they're telling him something.

Now that we have an idea of how many people are buying guns, let's look at the number of gun-related crimes and how they correlate with the number of guns purchased. The Washington Post reported data from John R. Lott, Jr. that stated, on December 3, 2015 gun crime has been declining for about 20 years, except for high-profile shootings in Gun-Free Zones; those shootings have been on the increase. Surprise, surprise. According to the Centers for Disease Control and Prevention there were 7 homicides by firearm per every 100,000 Americans in 1993. By 2013 that number has been cut in half bringing the new total to 3.6 per 100,000. Non-fatal crimes involving guns (such as robberies) declined even further. In 1993 there were 725 per 100,000 non-fatal and only 175 per 100,000 in 2013.

Here are the numbers from 2009-2014 depicting the correlation between deaths in America involving guns and the number of gun purchase background checks by the National Instant Criminal Background Check System (NICS). The numbers clearly indicate that as more people purchase guns, the number of deaths involving guns goes down. This is due to the fact that good people are able to defend themselves. Can you imagine the death rates if only the criminals had guns?

Year	FBI reported firearm deaths	NICS background checks
2009	9,199	14,033,824
2010	8,874	14,409,616
2011	8,653	16,454,951
2012	8,897	19,592,303
2013	8,454	21,093,273
2014	8,124	20,968,547

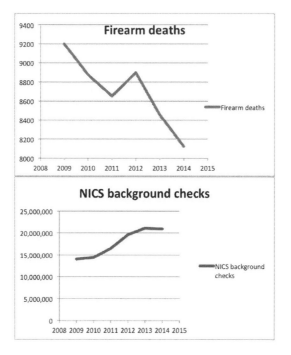

Gun ownership increased for 20 years as gun homicides decreased; except of course in Gun Free Zones. Is the decrease in crime coupled with the increase in firearm ownership a coincidence? The facts show that more guns in the hands of law-abiding Americans equals less crime, yet the rhetoric and false narrative from anti-gun politicians is the opposite. The Anti-2nd Radicals are kicking and screaming in the hopes of convincing the world that guns are bad and more restrictions should be implemented. If you didn't know the truth, you would think it's a war-zone out there. The problem is, many people don't know the truth. Many of those people are scared to death of guns and gun owners. Many of those people are single-issue voters and would gladly see your rights go away.

In all fairness to the Gun-Shamers, there is one area in which gun-related homicides have dramatically increased. You guessed it; the infamous Gun Free Zone. 2011 brought with it a new period in history which mass shootings occurred more often in places that had one thing in common; The Gun Free Zone. Some of the Gun-Free Zone killings between 2011 and 2015 include: the Aurora movie theater, Sandy Hook Elementary School, the D.C. Navy Yard, Arapahoe High School, Fort Hood, Emanuel African Methodist Episcopal Church, Chattanooga Military Offices, the Lafayette Grand Theatre, and Umpqua Community College. It's no coincidence that maniacs who want to kill the most people possible with the least amount of opposition seek out Gun Free Zones.

When mass-killings occur it seems that people take one of two approaches to fixing the problem. Anti-Gunners focus on the gun and want to see more restrictions. From a reactive mindset, that would makes sense, but it's important to look at the effects of those actions and see that restricting gun ownership with more laws only disarms the Good Guys. Gun owners on the other hand want to implement forms of protection for the innocent people who could potentially become victims in these gun-free killing zones, so we like the idea of putting people in place who are equipped to counteract the Bad Guy. It only makes sense to defend against a gun with a gun.

We are primarily fear driven creatures, which is why we develop new ethics and habits after a traumatic experience. We seem to make major changes only when push comes to shove and the stakes are increased. This is why the 55 year old, beer drinking, pizza eating, overweight guy will completely change his habits after having a heart attack. The fear of dying becomes a much stronger motivator than the satiation of consuming Super Bowl food on a regular basis. Prior to the heart attack he may have told himself his habits were not a problem so there was no need to change but the heart attack gives him a new reality. This is why there is always a big push to do something about mass shootings immediately after an incident occurs. Plus, the anxiety level in the people is high so the anti-gun rhetoric goes a long way. The best time to anchor a belief is when a person is in a heightened emotional state. People tend to be in a heightened emotional state immediately after finding out children in an elementary school were just gunned down. To an anti-gun politician there is no better time to ramp up the rhetoric. The problem is, lawmakers make the problems worse with gun restrictions and Gun-Free Zones because these policies affect good people in a negative way while empowering the killers.

Many people don't think firearm protection is necessary and they will even argue that it makes situations more dangerous. This is a thought process that stems from a lack of gun-knowledge, a fear of guns, and/or a fear of not being able to control gun owners. There are some rare cases when a person does experience a life-or-death situation involving guns and doubles down on the belief that a gun would not have helped. The way we think is subjective to our beliefs. Our beliefs are developed through the process of our life experiences.

In most cases when a person experiences danger from an attacker or criminal they rethink the idea of gun ownership and re-evaluate the validity of guns as life-saving devices. This is similar to the guy who has the heart attack and decides that eating healthy and exercising is now a good idea. When life becomes threatened and people realize how vulnerable we can often be, they look for the
226

most effective and logical ways to preserve their life. Gun ownership and often carrying are the go-to solution for most people; and with good reason. How else would you affectively protect yourself against someone with a gun? Beg for your life? Remind him he is in a Gun Free Zone? Call the cops?

The stories of people who came to the conclusion that gun ownership is a good idea after an incident are endless. I can't possibly document all of them but one in particular always stands out in my mind.

Suzanna Hupp is a woman who survived the 1991 mass shooting in Texas. She did not grow up around guns and did not agree with hunting but was given a handgun by a friend to keep in her purse so she could protect herself. Suzanna tells the story of how she was eating in a cafeteria with her parents one day when a maniac drove through the building and started shooting people. She explains how it takes one second to switch magazines in an attempt to show legislators how ineffective a ban on high capacity magazines would be.

When she realized that the madman's only purpose was to kill as many people as possible, she and her father got on the floor to try and save their own lives. Suzanna goes on to explain that in her moment of desperation she remembered that she had her gun in her purse and since the killer was only 12 feet away she felt it would be a reasonable chance to take him out and save lives. But lo and behold, due to current laws that would make Suzanna a felon for carrying, she had previously removed the gun from her purse. In fact she and her parents were completely unarmed and helpless. Suzanna was quoted as saying, *"My gun was out in my car, 100 yards away, completely useless to me, because I'd wanted to obey the law."* Suzanna's father decided to rush the madman and got shot in the chest. Suzanna then grabbed her mother and escaped the scene when she

227

had the opportunity but soon realized that her mother never followed her out. Her mother decided to return to her husband and hold him during his last minutes. The killer shot Suzanna's mother in the head. Both of Suzanna's parents died that day just after their 47th wedding anniversary.

Suzanna explained to legislators that being mad at the killer would be like being mad at a rabid dog. She also pointed out how the gun didn't walk into the cafeteria and pull its own trigger, focusing the attention on the actions of Legislators who created the law that took away her right to defend herself. She made it perfectly clear that she was in fact mad at her legislators for legislating her out of the right to protect herself and her family. During her speech, Suzanna went on to explain how important the 2nd Amendment is to the ability for protection against government.

Videos of Suzanna talking about the incident are very powerful and bring the reality of self-defense and the recognition of its importance to light. This is one of many cases where a person's appreciation for self-defense occurs after a deadly situation. It's not surprising that Anti-Gunners and Radicals can push forward with their agenda because most have never experienced a situation like Suzanna's. The fear of danger along with the inherent need to protect and preserve our own life is a powerful motivator. Many people just do not comprehend this human drive until they are involved in a deadly situation. That is why it is so important to help Anti-Gunners see the possibility that their lives may, too, be put in jeopardy sometime in the future and they may want to consider a semi-automatic life insurance policy.

The typical argument that Anti-Gunners and Radicals will use with a situation like this is that having a gun to protect yourself may make the situation worse because bystanders may get shot. Suzanna says, *"But I'll tell you the one thing that nobody can argue with; it sure as heck would've changed the odds."*

The anti-gun narrative is strong and although it is the voice of the minority, lawmakers and cheerleaders can make a lot of noise in support of all that is anti-gun. When lawmakers push for gun restrictions and laws that will supposedly prevent gun violence, they often use terminology that sounds pleasing to the average person. The words are carefully chosen in the hopes of swaying public opinion in favor of the latest violation they are about to implement. They will use terms like *"common sense* gun laws" and "The SAFE Act." The latest universal background checks being hustled by President Obama are part of a new push for what is being called "common sense gun laws."

You need to have a lot of faith in your government to support universal background checks. The anti-gun argument promotes the idea that criminals would be denied access to firearms therefore resulting in lives saved by a universal background check system. They argue there is no downside and that universal background checks are part of a "common sense" approach to stopping gun violence. They also state that 83% of gun owners and 87% of the general public would support this type of background check. The NRA and gun owners push hard against this for valid reasons that never seem to make an appearance in the mainstream media.

There are a few problems with the universal background check concept. For starters, the fees involved would put an extra burden on gun owners. For instance, if you wanted to give your grandfathers shotgun to your son he would be required to pay fees up to and sometimes above $200 and he would be required to go through a background check while the person gifting or selling the gun would have to become a licensed dealer. If someone were to gift a gun to a family member without going through this process, this new law would make them a felon. Next is the idea that my guns have always

229

been my business. Why would I want the government keeping track of my guns? They already know how much money I make and they make sure they take a fat chunk of it. You mean to tell me my guns are not at risk of an over zealous government? They also tell me how I will take care of myself and my family by regulating my health care options. If I choose not to comply and use the healthcare providers they determine are in my best interest, I am fined and penalized via my income (which they have control of). But somehow monitoring my guns for me will be different?"

Universal background checks also serve as a gun registry. Before the Obama administration you may have been considered a conspiracy theorist for thinking that the government was not working in the best interest of the people, but by 2016 it is pretty clear that government invasion of privacy is not only possible but something we now have a duty to fight to prevent. As usual, an argument for universal background checks may look like it makes sense on the surface, but like other so-called "common sense" gun regulations, as you dig deeper into the effects you start to see the real motives behind the masquerade.

Besides the costs involved, government having its nose in every single gun transaction in the country and the development of a national gun registry of law-abiding gun owners, the studies show that universal background checks do nothing to prevent gun crimes. The NRA reported that studies by the Federal Government show that people arrested for gun crimes typically did not get their guns through legal purchases. Nearly half of illegally trafficked guns were acquired through straw purchasers—people who can pass background checks and buy guns for criminals on the sly. No amount of background checks can stop these criminals. And as I said, this practice is illegal already. A miniscule amount of straw purchases are investigated unless a violent crime is ultimately committed with the gun purchased for the prohibited person. The law is on the books already regarding straw purchases. We need to enforce the laws we have, not create more laws which do nothing to curb violence. Universal background checks equal national gun registry and ultimately gun confiscation.

I often hear the argument for an Australia–like gun-free society here in America. Anti-Gunners seem to believe that Australia turned into Utopia after the government issued a gun ban. They either think people don't have access to the true results or they have been bamboozled by their liberal-progressive political leaders and given completely false data. The truth about Australia's buy-back or gun confiscation (whichever you prefer) is that it was a dismal failure. The government buy-back and registration list that started in 1996 and the handgun ban in 1997 showed opposite results of what Hillary Clinton and other anti-gun politicians in America would like you to believe. One year after the Australian ban it was determined by a Harvard study that Australian "suicides by gun" went down by 57%. But the suicide *rate* reached a ten-year high. This tells us that although people had less access to guns, it did nothing to deter suicides. As a matter of fact, they increased. Anti-Gunners only recite the 57% reduction in "suicides by gun" because that part fits their narrative.

While Australia's rate of violent crime has peaked in the years following its ban, the United States experienced the exact opposite phenomenon. One year after gun owners in Australia were forced by law to surrender their 640,381 personal firearms, (which were destroyed) new statistics were calculated. The mandatory gun buy-back program cost Australian taxpayers over $500 million dollars and resulted in a 3.2% increase in homicides, 8.6% increase in assaults and a 44% increase in armed robberies. These are the policies our Democratic politicians want you to embrace and they will use any and every tactic available to them to convince you to support them.

231

Hillary Clinton mocking and making fun of Americans concerned about gun confiscation said,

"People get scared into thinking that a black helicopter is going to land in the front yard and somebody is going to take your guns."

Another area that should be addressed when we talk about lies from Anti-Gunners is the Hollywood effect and the idea that guns go off by themselves. I want to debunk the Hollywood myth that when a gun is dropped it goes off. You've seen it a million times in movies. The best scene of a gun with the mind if it's own is in the movie "True Lies." This is where Jamie Lee Curtis' fully automatic MAC-10 falls down a staircase and kills everyone in sight on its way down. As it falls down the stairs in slow motion it sprays bullets every time it hits a step. The gun also rotates and moves from side to side in the air while it's falling to cover a wider span of the room. This is a perfect example of the false narrative and fantasy imagery Anti-Gunners use to get a negative reaction out of people who don't know any better. Watch this scene on YouTube and you'll understand the impression that is intended by this completely ridiculous scene. The scene is hysterical but scary because we see the intent behind it. Not only is an automatic weapon used in the scene, but also the magnificent way in which the gun kills people all by itself makes it the perfect propaganda piece.

When some people see things like this over and over, they believe it to be true. These images are powerful and although logic tells us it may be unrealistic, the mind still holds the image. These images help form our beliefs. Our beliefs influence our thoughts and our thoughts influence the things we say and do. That's just how we operate. Some people cannot decipher reality from fiction and this can result in a continued stream of falsehoods by the press when it comes to guns. A perfect example is the quote by Kristen Rand of the Violence Policy Center. Kristen said, *"Teddy bears get tested to*

232

make sure they can withstand use and abuse by kids, but guns don't get tested to make sure they don't go off when accidentally dropped."

Kristen's quote wouldn't be so bad if it were true but the truth is guns *are* tested for accidental misfire. In 2001 California required all handguns manufactured or imported into the state be drop tested. Drop Tests were also included in the federal Gun Control Act of 1968 for all imported guns.

In addition to required drop testing, there are a number of safety features installed in firearms to further prevent misfires. Some of them include:

- Thumb safety
- Trigger safety
- Grip safety
- Hammer safety
- Glock Safe Action System
- Firing pin block
- Hammer block
- Transfer bar
- Safety notch
- Magazine disconnect
- Decocker

An additional "safety feature" that gets a bit of controversy is the "long hard trigger press" such as the NY1 8lb trigger and the NY2 12lb trigger. Some law enforcement officers are required to use these heavy triggered guns. The common complaint is that accuracy is greatly diminished and some even argue that this attempt at making guns safer is not an improvement but a dangerous feature because it compromises the accuracy of the shooter.

So although it is possible for some guns to "go off" when dropped it is highly unlikely and the point here is to make sure the rhetoric and lies be countered with truth. In many respects guns are safer than they have ever been and manufactures are consistently testing and improving their products despite the misrepresentations you hear in the media and see in the movies.

Throughout this book we've talked about the lies, the false narrative, the overall misleading nature in which guns in America are often portrayed and the endless attempts that are made to chip away at the rights of gun owners. The way in which anti-gun politicians go about their mission to make legal gun ownership difficult is deceiving and dangerous.

Typically when negotiating, there are benefits for both parties involved. You know, "I want this, so I'll give you that." I often hear the argument from anti-gun activists and Anti-2nd Amendment politicians that gun owners are unwilling to compromise on or accept the litany of restrictions and proposals they have brought to the table. Well, that's true. Gun owners are not willing to compromise or accept the policies, restrictions or laws Anti-Gunners dream up that have proven to be ineffective and do nothing to get to the cause of the violent behavior we deal with on a regular basis here in America. Should the anti-gun politicians accept their position in the argument by admitting that they are obligated to uphold the 2nd Amendment and pursue the laws that are already in place, America would be a much safer place.

We have seen the destructive ways restrictions on gun use limit law-abiding citizens and embolden criminals. We recognize that laws are currently in place to incarcerate criminals for using guns to commit crimes, yet the prosecutions are not fully enforced. We know that government has the ability to put mentally ill people in the NICS database to prevent them from purchasing guns, yet they refuse to do

234

so. We are aware of many cases in which criminally unqualified people attempt to purchase guns and are not even arrested. There are many ways in which our government can enforce the laws already in place and take advice from the professionals like the NRA, however they seem to be primarily focused on pursuing the battle against the Good Guys.

Pro-gun advocates would come out in droves to support a government that was truly working on behalf of the people. Many gun owners would encourage things like firearms training courses offered in schools, armed security guards at schools, the elimination of "Gun Free Zones," gun ranges in State parks, the ability to freely carry in public and the enforcement of the laws already on the books but we will not allow a seat at the negotiating table to anyone who seeks to do harm to or restrict the rights of the people. Plenty of ways to reduce violent behavior with guns are available. When efforts are put toward those ends the gun community will come out in support. Ridiculing, discrediting, demonizing and restricting law-abiding gun owners are not tactics that will gain the Antis a viable voice in the conversation and they will not be tolerated.

So you have to wonder, amidst the list of logical solutions that go unused, what is the real end-game for anti-gun activists? This is the real problem we face because it will very much affect the future freedom of all Americans. It would seem that the efforts are focused on controlling the people under the guise of "public safety," but you already knew that. The question is what are we willing to do about it?

There are between 300,000,000 and 350,000,000 guns in America. The number is debatable because accurate data is not available and we'd like to keep it that way. That's about 1 gun for every person. Some estimates say there are over 350,000,000 guns in our population of approximately 319,000,000 people. The point is, firearms are not a passing fad and not something we are willing to give up. Firearms are a big part of our culture. The idea that some would denounce them and consider them inconsequential to our American lifestyle and freedom is preposterous. To blame violence on guns and not put the focus on human behavioral issues is irresponsible, destructive and quite possibly an excuse to execute an ulterior motive. Guns don't need to be fixed. People need to be fixed.

It's a frustrating conversation to have because we have otherwise intelligent people fighting to make sure the world maintains a strong focus on the gun while ignoring the real cause of deaths in America. On one hand you have the gun, knife, car, rock, hammer and any other tool that can be used for good or bad. On the other hand you have angry, destructive, deranged people using those tools to kill others. Fixing the cause of the problem (violent human behavior) *should* be at the top of everyone's priority list but those problems run very deep and the solutions seem impossible. Destructive psychological human behavioral issues run so deep that most people don't want to touch the subject. Since people need to feel good about their work and have a sense of accomplishment, they collect all sorts of data justifying how dangerous guns are. It's a very misleading game they play and it is very difficult to put your finger on the strategies they use because the strategy is to deter focus from the problem. The goal is to keep the real problem out of sight. By making everyone look at the gun it takes the attention off a deteriorating set of human ethics, morals and family values. This is where we should be focused.

The anti-gun lobby has set up the argument to keep the focus on statistics and laws. They want gun owners to be fully occupied in arguing over which restrictions are good or bad and which statistics are true or false because it keeps everyone's attention exactly where they want it - on the gun. This tactic keeps the focus off the fact that its their liberal-progressive, anti-gun policies that put people in danger and contribute to creating an unsafe environment. The real villains are those who try to disarm good Americans and make them helpless against criminals, but most people don't recognize that because they are too busy screaming about the "gun show loophole" or the number of rounds a magazine can hold. While redirecting the public's focus to gun laws and restrictions, the Anti-2nd Amendment Radicals simultaneously work at loosening the penalties for criminals and re-instate their voting rights. The real bad guys are the ones taking away your rights, creating Gun Free Zones and encouraging killers. The attention needs to be redirected at them. The spotlight needs to be shined in their face. They perpetrate the problem. Is it time yet to hold the Anti-Gun Radicals accountable and show the world exactly who they are, what they are doing and the deaths they are responsible for?

Had it not been for guns we would not even have the freedom to be talking about these things. Guns are the reason we have freedom. The gun is a tool we can use for many good things. The problem is our ignorance of basic human morals. You have a basic set of values and a moral standard when you walk into your home and interact with your family. Some of those who live among us have no parameters to define good behavior from bad. Our morals and ethics are what guide us internally. If those are not instilled in children, the problem compounds upon itself over generations. The opposite is also true. Those who are taught good behavior from bad and are given a set of moral standards to live by, grow up to instill the same values in their children. Those productive values also compound. This is why you see some families progress further and further as generation go on and some deteriorate. We are in a society where thoughtful, forward moving, loving people live together with immoral, destructive, careless people. We also have those who cannot see this logic and continue to propagate a false narrative. Therein lies the problem.

So the next time an Anti-Gunner tries to push smokescreen data on you and refuses to discuss the deterioration of human values and the rampant violent human behavior we have in the world, ask them what they've done to fix the real problem. Ask them if they even know what the real problem is. Ask them how they can justify focusing on a Good Gun and not the Bad Guy.

The truth is, we don't have a gun problem in America, we have an anti-gun problem.

AFTERWORD

Throughout the battle to preserve our rights and safety, I often hear the same question from Anti-Gunners. They get angry when their hypocrisy is exposed and they will ask sarcastically, "How would *you* solve the problem of gun-violence?" My response is always the same. I don't know that I will ever have the answer to preventing mental illness, gang violence, radical religious murders, or vicious behavior which in fact are the problem. I have suggestions and have presented some of them in this book. I don't know that it's within my scope of expertise to figure out these problems of humanity. I'm sure there are much smarter people than I who can take on those issues. I do think that I have a responsibility to help preserve the rights of people to protect themselves because it would seem that the real issues are not being addressed effectively. Exposing the lies of those who want to make us unarmed and helpless is part of that duty.

I understand the fear and anger some have with guns but that does not justify their reactive, dangerous solutions. Understanding the thought processes behind their fear is the first step and I hope I have done my part in starting the conversation.

Thank you for reading and I hope in some way you are able to benefit from this book. Please share it with the ones you care about and feel free to contact me through the Good Gun Bad Guy website or blog.

Stick to your guns,

Dan Wos

www.goodgunbadguy.com
www.danwos.com
www.goodgunbadguy.blogspot.com

ABOUT THE AUTHOR

Dan Wos is an American entrepreneur, author, musician and NRA member. He is founder and President of three corporations—including House Detective Inc., a home inspection & appraisal company serving many markets across the United States. He is also an active real estate investor.

Wos has been a musician since the age of 9. He has toured extensively throughout the United States in live bands and has many published works to his credit, including the 2000 Iron Cat records release U.S.Bandit by U.S.Bandit, the 2006 Iron Cat Records release Voodoo Man by the Dan Wos Project and the 2014 book Defining Success in America published by Iron Cat Publishing and Balboa Press. Some of his music has been featured in TV shows, commercials and on radio in many countries around the world.

Dan frequently speaks in educational presentations on a variety of topics. He continues to record music write books and write commentary for blogs and websites.

Dan is also interested in graphic design, and collector cars (primarily Corvettes, of which he has had an extensive collection throughout the years). Dan lives with his wife and son in Saratoga Springs, NY.

RESOURCES

WEBSITES

www.goodgunbadguy.com
www.goodgunbadguy.blogspot.com
www.danwos.com
www.janmorganmedia.com
www.nra.org
www.zackssports.com
www.traininghousesaratoga.com
www.bestbytesmedia.com
www.johnrlott.blogspot.com
www.fbi.gov
www.cdc.gov
www.iihs.org